CHRISTIANITY 101 SURVIVAL GUIDE

CHRISTIANITY 101 SURVIVAL GUIDE

WHAT IS GOD'S HONOR "THAT IS " NECESSARY FOR THE MESSIAH, YESHUA, JESUS

STEPHEN KIRKENDALL

STEPHEN R KIRKENDALL

CHRISTIANITY 101
SURVIVAL GUIDE
WHAT IS GOD'S HONOR
THAT "IS NECESSARY" FOR
MESSIAH, YESHUA, JESUS?
AUTHOR: STEPHEN R KIRKENDALL
KNOWN AS: JESUS'S WOLF HUNTER

Library of Congress Control Number: 2023914782
ISBN 979-8-218-25930-3 (paperback)
ISBN 978-1-088-26707-3 (digital)

Dedication

With special thanks to Kathleen M Kirkendall; Rachelle; Heather; Eva; Taylor; Paige; Amy; Colton; Jaylynn; Rob; Jason; Michael Jr.; Jessey; Ashley; Jordan; Eiesland family, Edward; Carole; James, and all the rest of my extended family starting with Jenny.

In helping with this guide, I give special thanks to Lucky Gilbert for his effort and encouragement.

Together we (the Christian body) can always be right! Because we are part of the same body, if we do not agree, we will, with patience (love) keep coming together with more information so we can agree. **Especially since there is only one truth**. How can we disagree **about honor for the Son of God**? Someone has not seen the same picture. We all have heard about different witnesses to an accident that gave different information and or had different visual memories.

This is about God's honor, of which, the full knowledge is not being taught **by any** Christian/Religious leader. **It is**, I pray unknowingly, **discrimination** against all the poor! The ones that do not have money but have **time** while **not knowing** their **time** can be God's honor. It is God's honor when used rightly! The ones the Messiah, Yeshua, Jesus asked that we help! Do you really love Him with more than your mouth, (fruit/evidence)? **What hurts one in the body hurts all in the body**. The no **money poor are a very large part of the body**! There could be **so many volunteers for "kids' safety squads"** in schools **that we would (almost) never have to worry about the children again**! There are **so many things** that volunteer **time (no cost) can do**. Volunteering makes you part of something, helps us feel we belong. Adds to sense of worth.

This guide includes my previous book NECESSARY FOR JESUS 70 PROPHECIES 70 REWARDS with new material. Some comments about it were. This text puts to rest the debate as to whether tithing still applies to modern Christianity, makes this scary concept much more powerful and even approachable for the modern reader, **recommended as a study guide for church leaders and teachers**, will bless anyone who reads it, bursts the topic of wide open, and excellent look at what is necessary for Jesus. **The best book on tithing that I**

ever came across, a fantastic job of presenting answers honestly
and without bias, and candidly clears the air on the subject mired
in silence and confusion, insightful, well presented, well researched,
thought-provoking, and deep. It was tight but right, an amazing job,
God's done an amazing work of transformation in my heart in
tandem with reading this book, will make us understand Christianity
better, a powerful book, and it is one of the best books to enlighten
anyone even if you are not a Christian! This is the best book for
the new millennium.

   You, the person reading this, can win even more souls for the Messiah, Yeshua, Jesus! You are going to want your group to be blessed,
before you even finish the first half of this guide and the only way is for
each person to have their own copy, for review and no need to worry
about taking notes, in a group meeting. This will be the greatest
fund raiser you have ever or will ever have as the giving is not one
time, it continues at a higher level. That way, in one day, everyone
would know how valuable their time is. It is God's honor. Real
Christianity is very easy. At the close of the meeting ask how many
copies for their family and friends would they like. A great eternal
gift. They might even join your group! I pray this is the best evange-
listic tool you will ever use! Let us all come together in unity to give
our time/money (God's honor) to the Messiah, Yeshua, Jesus so He
will come back sooner!!!

   Heb 13:18-19 Pray for us (*we the body); for we are confident
that we have a good conscience, in all things desiring to live honor-
ably. But I especially urge you to do this, that I may be restored
to you the sooner. (Did you read what I just did? If we came together, He would come back sooner !!!). Now may the God of peace
who brought up our Lord Jesus from the dead, that great Shepherd of
the sheep, through the blood of the everlasting covenant, make you

complete in every good work to do His will, **working in you what is well pleasing in His sight, though Jesus Christ.**

When you're ready **please help** this message get out **by giving your review** to the company you bought this guide from!

TABLE OF CONTENTS

INTRODUCTION

This guide is just to help you get a good start, first grade! **When you become involved** with your **time** and or money by knowing how valuable your **time** is to God **you can grow in His power.** There are **many benefits once you become involved!** If you have no **time** and or money invested, it means very little to you! No fruit/evidence.

For thousands of years, **with so few having made it to heaven instead of everlasting fire(hell) for eternity,** why do we still except religion over Christianity? **God loves us so much** and so few could earn or obey the rules of religion, that He decided to have a Son and ask Him to pay for our sins. **Going to heaven is so easy now because the Messiah, Yeshua, Jesus said yes** and only asks that we help others. He always intercedes for us even when we screw up as **we keep trying to do it right.**

No other king has ever accepted for his honor as little as the King of Kings, the Messiah, Yeshua, Jesus. The other kings want material things for their honor. Whereas the King of Kings, the Messiah, Yeshua, Jesus **values your honor (time) helping others so much, that it is His Honor,** making **your time the most valuable asset you have. What could be more important than our Gods honor that "is" necessary for His Son the Messiah, Yeshua, Jesus!**

It appears to have **been hidden for the last two thousand years.** What "**is**" **necessary** for the Messiah, Yeshua, Jesus? It doesn't help that a perverted bible used by many currently, has (changed the message, the truth) about **God's honor that "is" necessary for His Son the Messiah, Yeshua, Jesus**, our risen savior, and best friend. Which bite out of that book contains the poison that could kill you. **Get rid of it! It is not worth the risk!** Again, please see chapter on which survival kit (Bible) later.

If you cannot acknowledge that it's all His by giving back 10%, through use of **your time** and or money, you will probably hear depart from me (Jesus), **which means go to hell**.

This is the place where I have lost too many of you. All of you that have called me crazy **now know** that I'm not talking about the Messiah, Yeshua, Jesus **lacking anything in Himself**. The person that spat in my face and the churches that have even walked me out of **their church**, over this, need to consider that **we are talking about God's honor**, that **is necessary** for His Son, the Messiah, Yeshua, Jesus and no one has ever proven me wrong with my use of scripture about the tithe. They would not even give me 5 minutes. **I offer $10,000 if I'm wrong about God's Honor**. You will be **very happy you can not win** when **you gain something of far more value.** More knowledge about God's honor that all denominations can agree about **if they would open their eyes!**

People who did many wonders and cast out demons will be told by Jesus to depart; I knew you not. They are going to hell! They thought they were Christians. How would a non-Christian even think they could get in?

90% of confessing Christians have been let down by our leaders! With the full truth **about God's honor being so easy**, how can we not **have one of the biggest explosions for the kingdom of heaven? Will they open their eyes?**

John 8:28-31 Then Jesus said to them, "**When** you lift up the Son of Man, **then** you will **know that I am Him**". **Since only 1 in 10 are giving God, His Honor, through His Son, we can't really say we know him, can we? **Good news is coming**!

Your eyes are about to be opened to **a truth hidden in plain sight** in the New Testament since it was first printed about 2000 years ago.

It **was necessary** by God's design that the Messiah, Yeshua, Jesus be born to die for our sins. The Messiah, Yeshua, Jesus fulfilled more than 70+ **different** prophecies that **were written down (recorded evidence)** over a **1,000-year's**, by 5 different Jewish prophets. The first by Moses, **all 70+ written down (recorded evidence)** in the Jewish Torah, which is the same as the **written down (recorded evidence)** in the first 5 books of the Christian Old Testament. I have been told there are over 100 prophecies that He fulfilled! 70+ are at the end of this wolf hunter's guide! They **ALL were fulfilled 500 years later**.

The Messiah, Yeshua, Jesus **is** who God's word says He is. **It is impossible that the Messiah, Yeshua, Jesus is not The Son of God.** He has only asked us to help others.

James 2:8 "If you really fulfill the royal law according to the Scripture, 'You shall love your neighbor as yourself,' you do well".

To encourage us, He gave us at least 70 different rewards, which I'm sure you will enjoy reading in later chapters for helping others in His name. They start in Matthew and go through Revelation. I really like the last two, **#69 says, have right to the tree of life, and #70 says, enter through the gates into the city**. Jesus, the Messiah, Yeshua is our risen savior and best friend. **I cannot understand why we didn't know** what **"is" necessary** for Him. It is so important that He uses 7 chapters of scripture to explain! **I cannot find any other teaching that uses this amount of scripture.**

Kingdom benefits for full tithing truth

Using the common sense that God gave this below average IQ, wolf hunter for Jesus, who almost flunked high school, GPA 1.2, who still can't spell or memorize, who spent too many hours in the corner of the classroom, never had to wear the pointed hat, who thanks God for tools that type and spell for us, **while learning I could read His word, why wouldn't the tithe be necessary?**

Kingdom benefits for teaching that tithing is necessary for Jesus, and necessary **does not** mean "under the law"! Think about this, the recipe currently being used is attracting only 1 out of 10. You **add** an ingredient, from the truth, the word, **which was already there, notice I didn't say take away**, and 2 out of 10 now like it! Only 2 is a 100% increase, I honestly believe that when the full truth about the tithe is taught **and who it Honors**, it will **encourage many more to give time and/or money**. There is no reason 10 out of 10 (1000% increase) will not help when they know the full truth, **or they're not saved, YET**! Most people being uncomfortable with strangers, if not already tithing will use money. With the use of the out of money (poor), the largest part of the body, their **time** volunteering, no money cost to have something done!

1. God receives His honor due to Him through His Son, the Messiah, Yeshua, Jesus.

2. God's Honor "**is**" necessary for His Son.! Heb 8:3 "**His Honor**" **bottom line is your time**!

3. Builds a much **stronger base for future growth**. When the value of my **time** really sinks in, **His power begins to show**!

4. There are too many people who are chased away because they feel Christian leaders beg **all the time** for money and leave churches that talk too much about money. There are church break ups and divorces over tithing, including myself, having gone through a divorce over the tithe. Her priest said I am crazy if I believe something is necessary for Jesus. **Just teach full truth** about the tithe from God's word and we learn what is "necessary" for our Savior,

5. **We will want to help with more money and/or time. How can we not want to, now knowing it is God's honor.**

6. Stop the savage wolves from devouring the sheep like they are doing on the Internet when they say tithing is not scriptural. **Stop them from saying pastors are thieves if they teach tithing**.

7. **Not speaking against, thereby suppressing knowledge, a perverted Bible is helping the wolves in their slaughter!** What does blood on your hands mean? **It must be bad since Paul cried 3 years night and day warning about it!**

8. God's workers get paid so they can afford to work.

9. The Messiah, Yeshua, Jesus "was" the perfect last blood sacrifice for sin. He cannot be replaced!

10. **Everyone needs and wants to belong to a group.**

11. What **God desires is our time**; he wants it to produce fruit—the **evidence** that goes with us. Since **time is money, everyone** who wants to serve the Messiah, Yeshua, Jesus can do so **without going into debt**! Nothing wrong with correct use of a credit card! Pay it off each month.

12. With more **time** and or money, we can have many more workers helping to expand the Kingdom. How many more souls will be saved? **A stronger base will bring new people!**

13. It only takes forty-eight minutes a day for six days. 4.8 hours a week to redeem your tithe owed on a 40 hour a week job. Your church knows who needs help. You can find a way to help someone for the Messiah, Yeshua, Jesus!

14. Can you imagine how many more people would be helped if **2 out of 10** tithed (**time** /money) instead of **only 1 out of 10**. I repeat, that is a 100% increase. With **time** use **we can have a 1000% increase.**

15. Would have funds for more children, widows, and anyone else needing help!

16. **We will not deny the good workers**, for fear the wolves will use it. It does not make sense to punish all the good workers for fear a bad one might use it.

17. Those that do not have an increase for one reason or another, **can still be counted in on being blessed**, as there are at least 70 different N.T. rewards for use of our **time**/money (God's honor)

18. **Really think and pray about this! If no time/money is invested, it means extraordinarily very little to you.** We give more attention to something that we put time and/or money into so **the more important it becomes.** We are reminded that everything is His in the first place.

19. James 2:8 If you really fulfill the **royal law** according to the Scripture, "You shall love your neighbor as yourself," you do well.

WARNINGS, (Over 25) Some with curses

One should have been enough. **Don't mess** with God's word! With so many warnings, God is telling us how serious His word is, while showing His love as any loving parent would that says don't touch, so the child **might avoid pain**! The New Testament refers to Scripture, the truth, it is written, the gospel or good news **more than 400 times**. How can we do as The Messiah, Yeshua, Jesus asked, **since we allow it to be changed**?

When was the last time you heard of someone getting out of a traffic ticket by saying they didn't see the sign, **especially a sign that has been there over 2000 years! But's** do not help either! **But** my church say's, **but** my pastor say's, **but** this big name tv person say's! **They don't** get you into Heaven.

Some of these are repeated though out this Jesus's Wolf Hunter's Survival Guide

Luke 9:26 For whosoever shall be ashamed of me **and of my words, of him shall the Son of man be ashamed**, when he shall come in his own glory, and in his Father's, and of the holy angels.

2 Tim 4:2 **Preach the word**; be instant in season, out of season; **reprove, rebuke, exhort** with all longsuffering and doctrine.

** **We must be ashamed of His words** since we **allow** them to be changed! Websters dictionary **reprove means** to express strong disapproval of **Rebuke means** to express sharp, stern disapproval of, **exhort means** to urge, advise, or caution earnestly; admonish urgently.

1 Peter 4:17-18 For the time has come for judgment to begin at the house of God; and if it **begins with us first, what will be the end** of those **who do not obey the gospel of God**?

John 4:23-24 But **the hour is coming**, and now is, **when the true** worshipers will worship the Father **in spirit** and **truth**; for the **Father is seeking such to worship Him**. 24 God is Spirit, and those who worship Him **must** worship **in spirit** and **truth**."

1 Cor 12:26 And if **one** member **suffers, all** the members **suffer** with it; or if **one** member is **honored, all** the members rejoice with it.

2 Cor 2:17 For we are not, **as so many, peddling the word of God**; but as of sincerity, but as from God, we speak in the sight of God in Christ.

Rom 1:18-21 For the **wrath of God** is revealed from heaven against all ungodliness and unrighteousness of men, **who suppress the truth** in unrighteousness,19 because what may be known of God is manifest in them, for God has shown it to them. 20 For since the creation of the world His invisible attributes are clearly seen, being understood by the things that are made, even His eternal power and Godhead, **so that they are without excuse**, 21 because, **although they knew God**, they **did not glorify** Him as God, **nor were thankful**, but became futile in their thoughts, and their foolish hearts were darkened.

John 6:27 Do not labor for the food which perishes, **but for the food which endures to everlasting life**, which the Son of Man will give you, because God the Father has set His seal on Him."

John 8:31-32 Then Jesus said to those Jews who believed Him, "**If you abide in My word**, you are My disciples indeed.

32 And you shall know the truth, and **the truth shall make you free.**"

Matt 4:4 But He answered and said, "It is written, 'Man shall not live by bread alone, but by **every word** that proceeds from the mouth of God."

Matt 7:15 "Beware of false prophets, who come to you in sheep's clothing, but **inwardly they are ravenous wolves**.

Matt 7:21-23 "**Not everyone** who says to Me, 'Lord, Lord,' shall enter the kingdom of heaven, **but he who does the will of My Father** in heaven.

22 **Many will say to Me** in that day, 'Lord, Lord, have **we** not **prophesied in Your name, cast out demons in Your name**, and **done many wonders in Your name?**'

23 And **then I will declare to them, 'I never knew you;** depart from Me, you who practice lawlessness!'

What have you done? **They who cast out demons and did many wonders **are going to Hell.**

Matt 10:32-33 "**Therefore whoever confesses Me before men, him I will also confess before My Father who is in heaven**.

33 **But whoever denies Me before men, him I will also deny before My Father who is in heaven**.

The tithe (honor-**time/money**) is the main way to confess Jesus before men! If you do not respond to what is necessary for Him, since it's God's honor, not under the law, you really need to get serious. **Why risk going to hell?** It's your choice!

Matt 13:14-15 And in them the prophecy of Isaiah is fulfilled, which says: 'Hearing you will hear and shall not understand And **seeing you will see and not perceive**; For the hearts of this people have grown dull. Their ears are hard of hearing, And **their eyes they have closed, Lest they should see with their eyes and hear with their ears**, Lest they **should understand with their hearts and turn, So that I should heal them**.'!!!!!!!

Matt 15:8-9 "These people draw near to Me with their mouth And honor Me with their lips, **But their heart is far from Me.**

9 And **in vain they worship Me**, Teaching as doctrines the commandments of men.'"

2 Cor 8:13-15 For I do not mean that others should be eased and you burdened; **but by an equality**, that now at this time your abundance may supply their lack, that their abundance also may supply your lack — **that there may be equality**. As it is written, "He who gathered much had nothing left over, and he who gathered little had no lack."

Col 1:28-29 Him we preach, **warning every man** and teaching every man **in all wisdom, that we may present every man perfect in Christ Jesus**. To this end I also labor,

Col 2:20-23 Therefore, if you died with Christ from the basic principles of the world, **why, as though living in the world, do you subject yourselves to regulations** — 21 "Do not touch, do not taste, do not handle," 22 which all concern things which perish with the using — according to the commandments and doctrines of men? 23 These things indeed have an appearance of wisdom in **self-imposed religion, false humility, and neglect of the body, but are of no value against the indulgence of the flesh.**

Titus 1:16 They profess to know God, **but in works they deny Him**, being abominable, disobedient, and disqualified for every good work.

Titus 2:1 But as for you, **speak the things which are proper for sound doctrine**.

James 2:10-11 For whoever shall keep the whole law, and yet **stumble in one point**, he is guilty of all.

James 5:19-20 Brethren, if anyone among you **wanders from the truth**, and someone turns him back, 20 let him know that he who turns a sinner from the **error of his way will save a soul from death and cover a multitude of sins.**

1 Peter 2:17 Honor all people. Love the brotherhood. Fear God. **Honor the King**.

1 Peter 4:7-8 But the end of all things is at hand; **therefore, be serious** and watchful in your prayers.

8 And above all things **have fervent love** for one another, **for** "**love will cover a multitude of sins.**"

Rev 22:18-19 For I testify to everyone who hears the words of the prophecy of this book: **If anyone adds to these things, God will add to him the plagues that are written in this book**; 19 and if **anyone takes away** from the words of the book of this prophecy, **God shall take away his part from the Book of Life**, from the holy city, and from the things which are written in this book.

Matt. 25:32–40 All the nations will be gathered before Him, and He will separate them one from another, as a shepherd divides his sheep from the goats. And He will set the sheep on His right hand, but the goats on the left. **Then the King will say to those on His right hand, "Come, you blessed of My Father, inherit the kingdom prepared for you from the foundation of the world**: for I was hungry and you gave Me food; I was thirsty and you gave Me drink; I was a stranger and you took Me in; I was naked and you clothed Me; I was sick and you visited Me; I was in prison and you came to Me." Then the righteous will answer Him, saying, "Lord, when did we see You hungry and feed You, or thirsty and give You drink? When did we see You a stranger and take You in, or naked and clothe You? Or when did we see You sick, or in prison, and come to You?" And the King will answer and say to them, **"Assuredly, I say to you, in as much as you did it to one of the least of these My brethren, you did it to Me."**

Which one of the goats is or was your friend, child or grand-child that didn't get full truth message?

John 14:23–24 Jesus answered and said to him, "If anyone loves Me, he **will keep My word**; and My Father will love him, and We will come to him and make Our home with him. **He who does not love Me does not keep My words**; and **the word which you hear is not Mine but the Father's who sent Me."**

Rom. 15:4 For whatever things **were written** before **were written for our learning**, that we through the patience **and comfort of the Scriptures might have hope.**

Heb. 6:9–12 **But, beloved, we are confident of better things concerning you, yes, things that accompany salvation**, though we speak in this manner. For God is not unjust to forget your work and labor of love which you have shown toward His name, in that you have ministered to the saints, and do minister. And we desire that each one of you show the same diligence to the full assurance of hope until the end, **that you do not become sluggish**, but imitate those who through faith and patience inherit the promises.

Matt. 26:54 But how then shall the scriptures be fulfilled,

**If they change??

Matt. 26:56 But all this was done, **so that the scriptures of the prophets might be fulfilled.**

Over 25 warnings to help us, **out of His love, to save us from pain** like a loving parent would advise not to touch fire!

Which survival kit (Bible)

I thank God for directing me to the KJV- KING JAMES VERSION with AMPLIFIED VERSION on the same page, so that if I was not sure, on the very same page was the Amplified verse to help me understand.

On a Google search for the question, what's wrong with the Amplified Bible, the answer, was the Amplified Bible has been viewed as being guilty of illegitimate totality transfer by giving multiple potential meanings of the word in a particular passage, readers "may" incorrectly conclude that multiple meetings of the word may apply regardless of the one which context would suggest. Having the Amplified on the same page of KJV has really been of help in clarifying when I was not sure in KJV.

The next question, how reliable is the Amplified Bible, answer. As far as accuracy goes, the opinion, **it is as accurate as any translation from Aramaic, Hebrew and Greek** to Latin, German and/or old English is going to get.

The multiple potential meanings in the Amplified **double checked on same page against the KJV you will** always have **the right answer.**

Wolf hunter's example, and those that I offend by my example please forgive me, but the message is more important. In Websters dictionary the 4-letter word that starts with an s, to some it means human waste, **lies or exaggeration or nonsense** or it means I just screwed up, or it means a bunch of junk, **or that's not true.**

Another example happened too many times to me. I lost count of the number of people that called me crazy when I told them something was necessary for the Messiah, Yeshua, Jesus. The negative things they said to others so they also would not take time. You would have to wonder if they are going to heaven, they would not take 20 minutes to read part of Hebrews. I have forgiven all of them. During all that time. I kept wondering why they didn't think of, **what if, they have missed something about our Savior? Twenty minutes?**

The same word can mean something different to different people but **having the KJV right next to the Amplified on the same page, I know you will come up with the right answer**. For this guide I chose to save time by using the NKJV, NEW KING JAMES VERSION.

This dispels one of the biggest lies from Satan. If you feel you can't read the word, it is totally untrue **because if I can**, you can! Just the fact that **you are reading this proves to me you can read the Bible** and understand it!

I think you'll like this! Recently after about 20 years of not bowling, I decided to try again. A genuinely nice couple accepted me on their team. On the internet there was a picture of a cat that was in the air falling from the upper stands of a large Stadium. The cat had hung on as long as it could. People had seen it, spread a flag out and caught it safely! I asked my new friend on the team if she had seen it and her response was yes, and how did the cat get there in the first place!? Her husband agreed. I was thinking how blessed the cat was. Some would say one lucky cat! Like the same word can mean different things to different people, in this case different people **saw the same picture** and our **thoughts were different.** In this case, all of us were right!

Most of us are so busy putting out the fire that **we forget about putting out the cause** of the fire. Someone left the door open; **they didn't read** the sign that said please keep closed. **Do not change the sign, (the Word). Over 25 warnings(sign's).** Once the door opens because of partial or overlooked scripture, we wander around just like that cat not knowing who to trust. Then we get into a situation that we need help and need to hang on as long as we can. I know I've said it before, but **the Lord says to hang on till the end at least 50 times in Scriptures**. While the cat was hanging on as long as it could, it gave time for people to see that it was in trouble. During that time, people were able to let others know and I'm sure some of them prayed.

Can you imagine the backup that would happen if you saw a police vehicle near a 55 mile per hour sign that had one of the five's painted white, it's there but you can't see it making it a partial sign? Some people would hit their brakes for fear of a ticket and cause a bad accident, others would just slow down to make sure the sign is right or needs repair. The officer was not even there to check for speeding!

If you use the perverted NIV, you could take this opportunity to review your notes and transfer them to your new KJV with Amplified Bible on same page or NKJV.

What a blessing it will be for you to review your notes when you transfer them, as they must've been important to you when you wrote them down!

With over 25 warnings, one should have been enough, **by "not" speaking against,** the perverted NIV, **you are helping to suppress the truth** which **brings God's wrath** (Rom 1:18). **You are feeding someone you know to** a very savage wolf. Why even think about keeping it (any perverted bible) They really sinned **when they changed message about God's honor. Why worry about what else they changed?** If you need more proof, try to find these scriptures in an NIV. Matthew 17:21,18:11, 23:14; Mark 7:16,9:44,9:46; Luke 17:36. Also many word changes that make a difference!? If they can't believe God's warnings what else do, they not believe?

***I believe we live in cursed times, because Leaders and Teachers have not stood up for the Messiah, Yahshua, Jesus's Unchanged Word.

If you use the perverted NIV New International Version all the following are wrong (???????)
in saying that something **is necessary, meaning needed today.** **These are the key words** in Heb 8:3 in each of the following Bibles. KJV King James Version; **it is of necessity.** AMP Amplified; **It is essential.** NKJV New King James Version; **it is necessary.** VUL The Latin Vulgate; **unde necesse est.** HNV Hebrew Names Version; **it is necessary.** The Geneva; **Of necessity.** CJB Complete Jewish Bible; **has to have.** WBT The Webster Bible; **of necessity.** WNT Weymouth New Translation; **must have.** WYC Wycliffe; **it is needed.** Tyndale; **it is of necessitie.** YLT Young's Literal Translation; **necessary, that He may offer.** Interlinear Bible; **it is of necessity.** ASV American Standard Version; **It is necessary.** BBE Bible In Basic English; **It is necessary.** WEB World English Bible; **it is necessary.** NAS New American Standard; **it is necessary.** NLT New Living Translation; **must make.** DBY The Darby Translation; **it is needful.** GNT Good News Translation; **must also have.** Wuest NT; **it is necessary.** NCV New Century Version; **must also offer.** Weymouth; **must have.** ESV English Standard Version; **is it necessary.** RSV Revised Standard Version; **it is necessary.** Greek; **of necessity.** Hebrew; **Wherefore necessary.** The Sar Shalom Hebrew-English bible; **it is necessary.** The Holy Aramaic Scriptures; **also has something.** Stong's; **important to have.** Abarim (Greek/English); **necessary to have.** The newer versions of Greek to English **all say they used same source to help,** other bibles like KJV, NAS and **most have added [it is].** How using the same source could a couple add [it was]? Read it without the [bracket, since that means it was not in the original] knowing we are talking about the existing priests, who die, and the new eternal High Priest's needs for today! The Codex Sinaiticus; **it is necessary.** The Catholic bibles say **it is necessary** or **necessity for** or **must have.**

Why risk God's wrath? Even your common sense tells you that maintenance (the tithe) is needed! **The tithe (your time/money) blesses God thru His Son the Messiah, Yeshua, Jesus.**

Acts 20:26-31 Wherefore I take you to record this day, **that I am pure from the blood of all men.** For I have not shunned to declare unto you **all the counsel** of God. 28 Take heed therefore unto your-selves, and to all the flock, over the which the Holy Ghost hath made you overseers, to feed the church of God, which he hath purchased with his own blood. 29 For I know this, that after my departing shall **grievous wolves enter in among you,** not sparing the flock. 30 Also **of your own selves shall men arise, speaking perverse things, to draw away disciples after them.** 31 Therefore watch, and remem-ber, "that by the space of **three years I ceased not to warn every one night and day in tears".**

There are way too many pastors and teachers with blood on their hands?!? This **is so serious** that **Paul spent 3 years night and day in tears warning the people!** They did not see the sign (in the word). No one has shown them, or they really are wolves. Either way,

    it hurts all of us in the body.

Never forget that God gave us His son for our forgiveness (1 John 4:10). **So, few had earned it through religion over thousands of years. God loves us so much that He had a Son and asked Him to be the final blood, sin sacrifice,** for everyone's sins. He did so much for us. The written (Recorded evidence) of the tithe shows that was it being done approximately 430 years before Leviticus added it into the law.

Lev 27:31 if a man wants at all to redeem "any" of his tithes he shall add one-fifth to it.

Time working is exchanged for money. Money can buy **time. Money and time are interchangeable!** Bottom line all the Messiah, Yeshua, Jesus has asked of us is that we help others! The tithe is still included in Leviticus law, for the religious Jews. And "**still continues**" for all His friends but not under the law!

Warning In Matthew and Luke, **it says "many" will say** to me (*Jesus) in that day, have **we** not **prophesied, cast out devils, done many wonderful works**, we have **eaten and drunk in thy presence** – thou hast taught in our streets and **the Messiah, Yeshua, Jesus says, depart I knew you not,** depart from me all you workers of iniquity.

**These are people who thought they were Christian, because why would a non-Christian be looking to get in? Please help stop as many as you can from burning in hell, by sharing the full truth.

This need repeating! More than 35 Bible's, Greek, Hebrew, and the Complete Jewish Bible (CJB) (which uses the words "has to have") and those three words are **used together nowhere else in that Bible**. Jesus uses the first 7 chapters of Hebrews to tell us how important the tithe is! Hebrew 8:3 says something "is" necessary for this one (*Jesus). **The perverted NIV has changed** the message **about God's honor** by changing Heb 8:3 ("is") to ("was") necessary. I say again it's easy to not notice that change, since there was something necessary for the Messiah, Yeshua, Jesus, His blood. In Hebrews 1 through 7, we are told that His blood is milk of the word, which of course we need, but to grow we need to have solid food that has also been talked about in Hebrews 1 through 7, that **accompanies salvation**, to prove we didn't use just our mouth!

I say again The New Testament refers to Scripture, the truth, it is written, the gospel or good news **more than 400 times**. How can we do as the Messiah, Yeshua, Jesus asked, **if we allow it to be changed**? **What Bible or denomination will your friends or children and grandchildren choose,** or have you chosen???? **Can you imagine the growth if 10 out of 10 helped with time and or money!!!!!!!!**

I repeat, even if only 2 out of 10, now gave, that is a 100% increase for God, if given to the Messiah, Yeshua, Jesus so He can give it to, His and our, Father God (John 5:23), **while building a stronger base** for the church growth which would automatically come from a stronger base. The more involved a person becomes, the more **they will involve friends and neighbors**.

HELP???????

Matt 23:37-39 **"O Jerusalem, Jerusalem**, the one who kills the prophets and stones those who are sent to her! **How often I wanted to gather your children together**, as a hen gathers her chicks under her wings, but you were not willing!38 See! Your house is left to you desolate; **for I say to you, you shall see Me no more** till you say, **'Blessed is He who comes in the name of the Lord!'"** Luke 13:34-35

The USA churches (parts) really need to step up their outreach/help to the Messianic Jews as they are the only ones that could reach enough Jews before we will hear "Blessed is he who comes in the name of the Lord! With this war, who knows what is next, even if somehow, they stop now (by our prayers) **we must look to the future**. Many will be killed today. **Not one of them** knew they were going to die today. Are you ready? It's too late when you die for, I wish I had known before **how easy real Christianity is**. We're spending all our time putting out fires instead of putting out the cause of the fires (crime) which of course is **lack of knowing** the Messiah, Yeshua, Jesus's Christianity, instead of men's religion.

Tithing is God's honor

According to Webster's *College Dictionary*, the tithe is, "a tenth of goods or income paid as a tax for the support of the church." According to the Bible, the tithe is a tenth of ***any* increase**.

What about the Old Testament law? The tithe was first introduced in the beginning of the Old Testament. In my years of working mostly with Christians, I had often heard that tithing was part of the Old Testament and is no longer required in the New Testament. When I hear someone say it's no longer required, I believe they have blood on their hands because they used partial Scripture, and **too many have assumed** since it's not required, it's no longer needed!

SO, WHAT, that it's not required or under the law, **it is still God's honor that is necessary for the Messiah, Yeshua, Jesus, His Son, so He can Honor, His/our, Father. John 5: 23**

Consider this: "Then Melchizedek king of Salem brought out bread and wine; he was the priest of God Most High. And he blessed him and said: 'Blessed be Abram of God Most High, Possessor of heaven and earth; and blessed be God Most High, Who has delivered your enemies into your hand.' And he gave him a tithe of "**all**" (Gen. 14:20).

Thank God that we have tried to stop slavery as people were included in this example as part of the tithe! This occurred approx. 430 years before the Leviticus law, when the tithe was added to it. How can something that came 430 years before the law be done away with (just because we are no longer "under the law") when it was not part of the law to start with? **The law included it, did not start it.** Offerings are also mentioned in the Old Testament, so does this mean that we should not offer them anymore? We know that the Messiah, Yeshua, Christ Jesus took the place of the sin offerings—the blood sacrifice—but He did not do away with the tithe, or freewill offerings.

I don't know about you, but I would like to continue to **rejoice in all I put my hands to.** I also want my **household to rejoice.** Which are **two of the 70 rewards, see later chapters,** for doing as the Messiah, Yeshua, Jesus asked! I have also been told that tithing was a Jewish practice and not applicable for Christians today.

Please consider this: God calls the Jewish people His chosen people, and we are grafted in when we accept the Messiah, Yahshua, Jesus as our Lord. It was considered a godly practice for the Jews, and we are now grafted in with the Jews, why would it not be a godly practice for us today? Tithing is even more important today, **especially when you consider *who* is being honored**! Both the Messiah, Yahshua, Jesus and God our Father.

I repeat, the Bible shows there are at least 70 spiritual rewards (see later chapters) that can result from giving beyond the duty of the tithe. Why would anyone risk losing even one of these spiritual rewards? **Why would it no longer be necessary for the maintenance of God's workers** when all that changed was there are no longer blood sacrifices for sins, which the Messiah, Yeshua, Jesus did away with by His blood sacrifice?

The 1 in 10 who tithe are doing it out of love for Jesus, and there can be no better reason. What if you also knew that it "is" necessary for the Messiah, Yeshua, Jesus, your best friend!

You who tithe are the **ones the Messiah, Yeshua, Jesus** has a bone to pick, **He said you should be teaching** *those who are still on milk.* By not teaching you are disobeying! Remember He even had a bone to pick with the church at Philadelphia that he loves, **as he also loves you!**

I'm so tired of hearing, but I teach tithing?! With the national average being that less than 1 out of 10 are tithing, it should be obvious that **something in the teaching has been missing**! In school you had to get 7 out of 10 right to pass!

Too often I hear **my church** really has good tithing. **Then why** are you not teaching other pastor's and teachers for the Messiah, Yeshua, Jesus **as He asked**? *They need the solid food of God's Word, which is the only way to stop* **the wolves from lying about tithing** which is (your **time**, God's Honor) and calling good teachers, and pastor thieves! There is way too much on the Internet and YouTube against tithing. If you are merely using your mouth to proclaim that you're a Christian while not honoring Christ by doing what He did, I must question your love for Christ? **The only way you can truly proclaim your love for Christ is by obeying and following Him.**

In Luke 6:46 The Messiah, Yeshua, Jesus said, "But **why do you call Me** 'Lord, Lord,' and **not do the things which I say?**".

In the verses at the end of this book's introduction, He is referring to the people who thought they could pick and choose the parts of the Scriptures that they were willing to obey. These same people are the ones who believe the wolf in sheep's clothing. The wolf tells them that tithing is not necessary for Christians today instead of what Jesus said.

Matt. 7:15–16 Beware of false prophets, who come to you in sheep's clothing, but inwardly they are ravenous wolves. You will know them by their fruits.

GOD'S HONOR (our time/ money) "IS NECESSARY" FOR THE MESSIAH, YESHUA, JESUS

This is the main point of the SURVIVAL GUIDE and should put an end to all lies and disagreements about the tithe (your **time**-His honor)

I must repeat this: No other king has ever accepted for his honor as little as the King of Kings (Yeshua, the Messiah, Jesus). The other kings want material things for their honor. Whereas the King of Kings (Yeshua, the Messiah, Jesus), **values your honor (time and or money) helping others so much, that it is His Honor**, making **your time the most valuable asset you have**.

What could be more important than our God's honor? Your eyes are about to be opened to **a truth hidden in plain sight** in the New Testament since it was first printed about 2000 years ago.

1 Peter 4:17-19 **For the time has come for judgment to begin at the house of God;** and if it begins with us first, what will be the end of those who do not obey the gospel of God? 18 Now "If the righteous one is scarcely saved, where will the ungodly and the sinner appear?" 19 Therefore let those who suffer according to the will of God **commit their souls to Him in doing good,** as to a faithful Creator.

John 5:22-23 For the Father judges no one, but has committed all judgment to the Son, **that all should honor the Son just as they** honor the Father. He who does not honor the Son does not honor the Father who sent Him.

Heb 1:1-4 God, who at various times and in various ways spoke in time past to the fathers by the prophets, 2 **has in these last days spoken to us by His Son**, ...when He **had** by Himself purged our sins, sat down at the right hand of the Majesty on high, 4 **having become** so much better than the angels, as **He has by inheritance** obtained a more excellent name than they.

*** There must be a death **before** there can be an inheritance! Hebrews is about Honor and reminds us of how much more worthy of Honor the Messiah, Yeshua, Jesus, is than angels and all the great Men and Women of God.

***note **Therefore** carries through each chapter, chapter 5 easy to see message carries through, up to Heb 8:4.

Heb 2:1-2 **Therefore** we must give the more earnest heed to the things we have heard, lest we drift away. 2 For if the word spoken through angels proved steadfast, and **every transgression and disobedience received a just reward**,

Heb 2:17-18 **Therefore**, in all things He had to be made like His brethren, that He might be a merciful and faithful High Priest in things pertaining to God, to make propitiation for the sins of the people. For in that He Himself has suffered, being tempted, **He is able to aid those who are tempted**.

Heb 3:1-6 **Therefore**, holy brethren, partakers of the heavenly calling, consider the Apostle and High Priest of our confession, Christ Jesus, 2 **who was faithful** to Him who appointed Him, as Moses also was faithful in all His house. 3 **For this One has been** counted worthy of more glory than Moses, 6 but Christ as a Son over His own house, **whose house we are if we hold fast the confidence and the rejoicing of the hope firm to the end.**

*****More than 50 times** scripture reminds us to hold on till the end. I believe this would be to show evidence of us not walking away!

John 6:66 From that time **many** of His disciples went back and **walked with Him no more.**

If you like to play with numbers, this verse 6:66 is bad when you think about a disciple that has and that more could walk away?!

Heb 3:9-10 And saw My works **forty years**. Therefore I was angry with that generation, and said, 'They always go astray in their heart, **and they have not known My ways.**'

Heb 3:18-19 And to whom did He swear that they would not enter His rest, but **to those who did not obey**? 19 So we see that they could not enter in because of unbelief.

Heb 4:1-2 **Therefore**, since a promise remains of entering His rest, let us fear lest any of you seem to have come short of it. 2 For indeed the gospel **was preached to us as well as to them**

***Those who say Hebrews was written only for the Hebrews can no longer say that!

Wolf Hunter's food for thought. What if it were written only for the Hebrews! Good news! The **Hebrews still are God's chosen people**. When we accept Christ as Lord in our life, we are grafted into the Hebrew vine!

Heb 4:11-13 Let us **therefore** be diligent to enter that rest, **lest anyone fall according to the same example of disobedience**. 12 For the word of God is living and powerful, and sharper than any two-edged sword, piercing even to the division of soul and spirit, and of joints and marrow, and **is a discerner of the thoughts and intents of the heart.** 13 And there is no creature hidden from His sight, **but all things are naked and open to the eyes of Him to whom we must give account.**

Heb 4:14-16 **Seeing** then **that we have a great high priest**, **that is passed into the heavens**, Jesus the Son of God, let us hold fast our profession. For **we have not** a High Priest which cannot be touched with the feeling of our infirmities; but was in all points tempted like as we are, yet without sin.

Let us therefore come boldly unto the throne of grace, **that we may obtain mercy, and find grace to help in time of need.**

Heb 5:1 For every high priest **taken from among men** is appointed for men in things pertaining to God, that he may offer **both gifts** and sacrifices for sins.

Heb 5:5-6 So also Christ glorified not himself **to be made a High Priest**; but he that said unto him, Thou art my Son, today have I begotten thee. 6 As he saith also in another place, Thou art a priest forever **after the order** of Melchizedek.

Heb 5:9-14 And having **been** perfected, **He became** the author of eternal salvation **to all who obey Him,** 10 called by God as High Priest "according to the order of Melchizedek," 11 **of whom we have much to say,** and **hard to explain,** since you have become dull of hearing. 12 For though by this time **you ought to be teachers,** you need someone to teach you again the first principles of the oracles of God; and **you have come to need milk and not solid food.** 13 For everyone who partakes **only of milk is unskilled in the word** of righteousness, **for he is a babe.** 14 But solid food belongs to those who are of full age, that is, those **who by reason of use** have their **senses exercised** to discern both good and evil.

*** Here is the start of the clues as to what "is necessary" for Jesus!

1. Much to say about.

2. Hard to explain.

3. You are slow to learn

4. **You should be teachers.**

5. It's solid food.

6. Reason of use, learning to discern good and evil through helping others! It takes **time** that is used and exercised.

Lev 27:31 If a man wants at all to redeem any of his tithes, he shall add one-fifth to it.

*** This Wolf Hunter for Jesus, thinks these needs repeating, is told all the time, but I teach tithing! If your church tithing is so high,

why are you not sharing with other pastors what makes it so good? I thought we all served the same Son of God, His Son the Messiah, Yeshua, Jesus? **If you are not teaching that the tithe** (part of the gifts) is necessary for Jesus as part of the evidence, that **accompanies** salvation (It doesn't earn salvation) and that the tithe can be redeemed with our **time**, which was exchanged for money, for the tithe, in the first place, **you are using partial scripture.**

The scripture says you have blood on your hands. (Acts 20:26-31)

Maybe this will help those that **cut me off** after telling me **that it is no big deal**, is or was!

Try this, the Messiah, Yeshua, Jesus **is dead** instead of **was dead!** I hope that really made your stomach turn.

WARNING! Gal 1:6-9 I marvel that you are turning away so soon from Him who called you in the grace of Christ, **to a different gospel,** 7 which is not another; but **there are some who trouble you and want to pervert the gospel of Christ**. 8 But even if we, or an angel from heaven, preach any other gospel to you than what we have preached to you, **let him be** 9 As we have said before, **so now I say again, if anyone preaches any other gospel to you than what you have received, let him be accursed.**

** Within 60 years of the **Messiah, Yeshua, Jesus proving He is the Son of God**; by raising from the grave, some were **already perverting** His word!?These needs repeating, scripture refers to the Scripture, the truth, the gospel, the word, and the good news **over 400 times so it is extremely important** that we do not change what it says.

There is a beautiful golden green frog so small that it could sit on your finger. Named the Golden Poison Frog that has enough poison to kill two bull elephants or for you anti mice people one could kill 20,000 mice! Why risk?

The poison from shingles can be in your body for 50+ years before the bad shows up!

Warning! 1 Cor 12:25-28 but that the members should have the same care for one another. 26 And if **one** member **suffers, all** the members **suffer** with it; or if **one** member is **honored, all** the members **rejoice with it**. 27 Now you are the body of Christ, **and** members individually.

Heb 6:1-3 **Therefore, leaving** the discussion of **the elementary principles of Christ**, let us **go on to perfection, not laying again the foundation of repentance** from dead works and of faith toward God, 2 of the doctrine of baptisms, of laying on of hands, of resurrection of the dead, and of eternal judgment. 3 And this we will do if God permits.

** Never forget the milk but grow up!! If we quit after elementary school, can you imagine what you're going to miss.

We have been told by the Messiah, Yeshua, Jesus **that there is something so important** that He **refers to faith toward God, of the doctrine of baptisms, of laying on of hands, of resurrection of the dead and of eternal judgment** as elementary!!!!

Heb 6:9-12 But, beloved, we are confident of **better things** concerning you, yes, **things that accompany salvation**, though we speak in this manner. 10 For God is not unjust to forget your work and labor of love which you have shown toward His name, in that you **have ministered to the saints, and do minister**. 11 And we desire that each one of you show the same diligence **to the full assurance of hope until the end**, 12 that you do **not become sluggish**, but imitate those who through faith and patience inherit the promises.

Heb 6:18-20 That by two immutable things, in which it was impossible for God to lie, we might have a strong consolation, who have fled for refuge to lay hold upon the hope set before us: 19 Which hope we have as an anchor of the soul, both sure and steadfast, and which entereth into that within the veil; 20 Whither the forerunner is for us entered, **even Jesus, made** a High Priest for ever after the order of Melchisedec.

Heb 7:1-2 For this Melchizedek, king of Salem, priest of the Most High God, who met Abraham returning from the slaughter of the kings and blessed him, 2 to whom also Abraham **gave a tenth part of all,** first being translated "king of righteousness," and then also king of Salem, meaning "king of peace,

Heb 7:4 Now consider how great this man was, to whom even the patriarch Abraham gave a **tenth of the spoils.**

Heb 7:8 Here mortal men receive tithes, but there He receives them, of whom it is witnessed that He lives.

****ONLY THE MESSIAH, YESHUA, JESUS HAS BEEN WIT-NESSED TO LIVE, SO THIS HAS TO BE REFERRING TO the Messiah, Yeshua, Jesus IN HEAVEN

** At the same time, religious Jews are giving tithes to priests who die, and the Christians (His friends) are giving tithes (God's honor, your time/money) to the Messiah, Yeshua, Jesus through His workers, for His workers.

Heb 7:15-17 And it is yet far more evident if, in the likeness of Melchizedek, there arises another priest **who has come**, not according to the law of a fleshly commandment, **but according to the power of an endless life**. For He testifies: "You are a priest forever According to the order of Melchizedek."

Heb 7:23-26 Also there were many priests, because they were prevented by death from continuing.

But He, because He continues forever, has an unchangeable priesthood. **Therefore, He is also able to save to the uttermost those who come to God through Him,** since **He always lives to make intercession for them**. to this day, I continue to thank God for bringing to my remembrance, Verse 25 when I needed it for my grandmother.

Being of American Indian descent, which I am immensely proud, she was raised for the first eight years of her life on the Nez Perce reservation in Idaho.

One Friday night, I called my grandmother and asked her if there was anything that she would like me to pick up for her and if she had time, I would like to talk with her in the morning. Of course, she said yes.

That night, it seemed like I kept getting busier and busier, and almost called my grandmother to delay my visit. When I arrived that Saturday morning, I can still see my grandmother sitting across the living room where she immediately asked me what I wanted to talk about. I asked my grandmother if she had ever received Jesus. She replied do you mean the white man's God. I replied of course not grandma, you know better than that. Then she asked me if I was perfect? Grandma, you know I'm not, I replied. Then the Holy Spirit prompted me to ask her if she had ever heard that Jesus lives to intercede for those who come to him. She answered yes. **If we were perfect, I told her, he would not need to intercede for us.**

She accepted Jesus that Saturday morning.

She died on Monday morning before I could make it to the hospital. She entered our eternal home in heaven because Jesus interceded for her.

He will intercede for you also!

Heb 7:26-28 For such a High Priest was fitting for us, who is holy, harmless, undefiled, separate from sinners, and **has** become higher than the heavens; 27 **who does not need daily**, as those high priests, to offer up sacrifices, first for His own sins and then for the people's, for this He **did once for all when He offered up Himself**. 28 For the law appoints as high priest's men who have weakness, **but the word of the oath, which came after the law**, appoints the Son who has been perfected forever.

Heb 8:1-4 **Now this is the main point of the things we are saying**: We **have** such a High Priest who **is seated** at the right hand of the throne of the Majesty in the heavens, 2 a Minister of the sanctuary and of the true tabernacle which the Lord erected, and not man. 3 For every high priest is appointed to offer **both** gifts and sacrifices. **Therefore, it "is" necessary that this One also have something to offer.** 4 For if He were on earth, He would not be a priest, since there are priests who offer the **gifts** according to the law.

Something is necessary for this one (*the Messiah, Yeshua, Jesus). It can only be the gifts, He took care of **the sacrifice**. One time for everyone. Of course, one of the gifts is the tithe! Is there anyone of you that would refuse to help your best friend if you knew something "is" necessary for him? **It's a lot easier than you think, with full truth!** ****So easy** because bottom line it comes down to **our time** which can buy money and/or money can buy **time**. We should have 100% tithing or if someone does not tithe (**time** and or money), they are not yet a Christian **and could face the ultimate bad news**. The full knowledge **stops the lies** about God's Honor. Those that say the tithe is not required, which leaves some to think not needed, should realize **so what,** not required, **it "is" needed**.

The word of God takes seven chapters (no other subject uses this amount of scripture) telling us how important Angels, Melchizedek, Moses and Abraham were, while reminding us **how much more** important **the Messiah, Yeshua, Lord Jesus is**. The only reason to be talking about Melchizedek was the tithe (Honor, time/money), the 10%. We are stealing Honor from God if we do not tithe, (Mal 3:8). The tithe is the only answer! The money and or time used for the workers is the only thing that could be necessary! (Evidence, your fruit).

Never forget that the Messiah, Yeshua, Jesus's purpose was and is for our forgiveness, while only asking that we help others and spread the Good News.

About 50 years ago a couple of versions decided to change "is" to past tense "was". What "was" necessary for Jesus. **Hard to argue about, way too easy to miss the change,** because something was necessary.

That is not the message here. How could you have accepted Christ without already knowing this? Even some unbelievers know. Milk of the word! He is the son of God. "Was" the perfect **last blood** sacrifice.

Using their own versions, it proves **they should not have changed scripture about God's Honor, which "is" necessary for Jesus. Which makes it perverted!** **perverted. Webster's College dictionary says it means **to lead astray morally, to turn away from the right course, to lead into mental error or false judgment, to turn to an improper use.**

If your version, only 3, that I found, one being the NIV, about 50 years ago, changed (Heb 8:3) "is" to "was". **It is a perverted book.**

This wolf hunter for Jesus, has been told, many times by pastors that they will not speak against the **NIV that has left out many verses and changed 1000's of words,** because **other pastors like it and a lot of their people like it!**

They are all afraid of losing members to a different pastor. I remind all of you who are **afraid of the big bad wolf** (you hirelings) that **you have helped bring curses on your flock** and please do not forget what a forgiving and loving God we have **when the light comes on.** God's wrath is not something to play with!

I prefer to believe the other 35 versions that I checked. **Aramaic, Hebrew, and Greek have stood for more than 2000 years,** KJV (1611) has stood for 400 years, Webster's 1833, if you can't believe the dictionary people on earth who can you believe, when it comes to translating?

The Complete Jewish Bible (CJB) that says, "has to have". Those are strong words that I could not find used together anywhere else in the entire Complete Jewish Bible (CJB).

What "is" necessary for my Creator (my eternal best friend)? He does not need my (oops it's His) money! How could He need anything?

Things that accompany salvation!!! (Heb 6:9).

Our obedience produces the fruit that accompanies salvation. **Evidence** we used more than our mouth! **Time** can replace (redeem) money (tithe)! Lev 27:31.

Your time was exchanged for money for the tithe in the first place!

In the beginning of the Old Testament, tithing was going on. About 430 years later it was included in the law. Tithing Is still in the law for religious Jews and continues at the same time, (not under law) for Christians today. Full New Testament tithing info **shows how easy it is to help.** God can not lie, right!

Matt 11:28-30 Come to Me, all you who labor and are heavy laden, and I will give you rest.

29 Take My yoke upon you and learn from Me, for I am gentle and lowly in heart, and you will find rest for your souls. 30 For **My yoke is easy** and **My burden is light."**

I repeat, **the good news** is that you get to review your notes when you transfer them to your new real bible.

Reminder, this wolf hunter for Jesus almost flunked High School so if I can read God's word, so can you. KJV with Amplified Bible combined, so if in the KJV I'm not sure, on same page is the Amplified to help, **it is my go-to**.

Yes, I like NKJV as this book shows.

When I looked at both versions together, I never found the Amplified wrong. It has always helped me to understand more when I needed to. Therefore, it's so important to consider the verses that precede. As for the scripture Hebrews 8:4 it can only be used to confirm what was summarized, **as the answers were already given**.

It is **also important to read the other scriptures pertaining to the same subject.** In the verses leading up to this point, it clearly talks about the tithe(honor) because that's what is meant by a tenth. The only reason Melchizedek was brought into this conversation was because of the tithe (honor) and to remind us that even though he was a great man, the Messiah, Yeshua, Jesus is even more so.

I do not know how God's Word could be read any differently, especially when you consider who it's for in Hebrews 8:3 and while remembering Hebrews 7:8. It said "them" (**the tithe) is for the Messiah, Yeshua, Jesus **so He has something to honor, His /our Father**. Furthermore, I believe that it will encourage you to give more than the tithe. It's "necessary" that the Messiah, Yeshua, Jesus "has to have," how can we consider giving him less than the old Melchizedek? **Our time can replace money, so nothing can stop me from honoring God!**

Will you continue to shortchange the Lord? Before you answer that question, consider this: What will be **your** (evidence) for the rewards here and in heaven? I am greatly concerned for anyone who says tithing is not for today! A wolf in sheep's clothing has led you astray willfully **or because he also has been led astray**. I repeat, when was the last time you heard of someone getting out of a traffic ticket by saying they didn't see the sign, especially a sign that has been there over 2000 years!

Why risk going to hell when you could have read for yourself instead of taking an opinion. It is bad enough for a person to lose his own rewards in heaven, but to cause others to lose theirs is much worse. What God says to do, we *must* do. We must help the ministry before it's too late.

When I checked the New Testament in other Bible versions, Hebrews 8:3 the words *necessary, essential,* and *needful* were used. The New King James Version uses the word *necessary*. Worth repeating, I found it very interesting that in the Complete Jewish Bible, the words *"has to have"* are used, and that phrase I could only find once in the whole Complete Jewish Bible.

He gave His life for us. How can we even think of giving Him less than what would've been given to Melchizedek?

Heb. 12:28–29 **Therefore**, since we are receiving a kingdom which cannot be shaken, let us have grace, by which **we may serve God**

acceptably with reverence and godly fear. For our **God is a consuming fire**.

Jude 4 For **certain men have crept in unnoticed**, who long ago were marked out for this condemnation, ungodly men, who turn the grace of our God into lewdness and deny the only Lord God and our Lord Jesus Christ.

Jude 16–19 These are grumblers, complainers, walking according to their own lusts; and they mouth great swelling words, flattering people to gain advantage. But you, beloved, **remember the words which were spoken** before by the apostles of our Lord Jesus Christ: **how they told you that there would be mockers in the last time who would walk according to their own ungodly lusts**. These are sensual persons, who cause divisions, not having the Spirit.

Jude 20–23 But you, beloved, **building yourselves up** on your most holy faith, **praying in the Holy Spirit**, keep yourselves in the love of God, looking for the mercy of our Lord Jesus Christ unto eternal life. And on some have compassion, making a distinction; **but others save with fear, pulling them out of the fire**, hating even the garment defiled by the flesh.

Jude 24–25 Now to Him who is able to keep you from stumbling, and to present you faultless before the presence of His glory with exceeding joy, to God our Savior, Who alone is wise, be glory and majesty, dominion and power, both now and forever. Amen.

Think about this, the Super Bowl ticket for eternal life **has been bought** for you. When you do not participate, what good is it? What if you go to the arena and sit in the lobby, you will miss every play. What if you sit in the arena and spend too much time on your cell phone or your iPad, you are going to miss a lot? Or if you spend too much time talking to the people around you, instead of watching the game, **their opinion of what the quarterback or coach should or should not have done is just an opinion!** Why did you even go?

<u>When you really watch</u> **(read the word) you will gain so much from that ticket being paid for you!!!**

Why Me?! JESUS'S WOLF HUNTER

I developed such a thirst for the answers to people's questions that, **I had to become Jesus's wolf hunter (like Paul)**. I kept thinking, *what a task it would be ,to study that much! Who am I? Why would anyone read what I have to say?* All my life I have heard the bible is hard to read! Reading the Scriptures, **I soon came to realize I could read the Bible** and I wasn't the one who was talking. I am merely presenting what God's Word has to say on the matter of God's honor, (your **time**/money). Copy & paste NKJV. Not my opinion!

In my studies, I learned that if we're not giving the Messiah, Yeshua, Jesus Christ what "is" necessary, essential, or needful or as, the Complete Jewish Bible (CJB) puts it—what Jesus "has to have" (and those words are only used together once in the entire version), **we may need to reevaluate our walk with the Lord.**

Tithing and other works do not earn our salvation (the Messiah, Yeshua, Jesus Christ has already paid that price for us), but they do serve as checkpoints where we can stop and ask ourselves, "Did I fully accept Christ as Lord? If so, **why am I not obeying His words**?" I pray that you do truly love the Messiah, Yeshua, Jesus and simply have not been shown or told the whole truth—what I call the shocking truth. Again, **I say "shocking" because the full truth has been in the New Testament for over two thousand years.**

For more than **thirty-five years**, I have helped 1,000's of people with money through mortgage loans, life insurance, investments, estate planning. For **twenty of those years**, I was on a live phone in Christian radio talk show. We did not screen callers. I had no idea what the questions would be. Here is a good laugh for you. You can now say you know the guy(me), that heard "Steve, they can't see you nodding your head on live radio"!

I was also a treasurer for many years with Full Gospel Businessmen. A group that helped **bring people from many different denominations together to reach the unsaved.**

I still can't believe how many of the, soon to be new Christians, **were amazed at how so many Religions** could be together! **Yes**, that is what the world thinks! It's a shame that some denominations really are! Our favorite saying was the labels will blow off on the way up or burn off on the way down. We all are judged by the same Messiah, Yeshua, Jesus.

I got to meet everyone who came as they bought their meal ticket from me. I also got to give free tickets to first timers that we paid for. I've been asked many theological questions about money. Please see chapters on a few, such as What is God's honor? What about the mark of the beast [666]?" "Can a Christian be wealthy; how should debt be handed" and "Isn't tithing just an Old Testament law that I don't need to practice?

Not being in ministry or raised in the church, **I was not looking though a veil, like pastors and teachers who only deal with their Group**. People from **many different denominations asked me questions**, which at first, I could not give a solid answer. I could not believe how many people said they didn't want to ask their group because of too many opinions. **I don't blame them as I cannot find one leader who teaches the full N.T. tithing truth. The full truth stops doubt and fear. Brings us together much stronger!**

I read books on Christian money management. I tore up the worst one before I threw it in the garbage. It tried to convince its readers that tithing is no longer scriptural and that anyone who taught so was "a thief"! When I looked up the verses the wolves quoted, I found that **all of them were changing words,** using only partial scripture, or the wolves used their own interpretation that did not match what the Word really says. Man's opinions **could help send you to hell**!

Obeying the Messiah, Yeshua, Jesus's words is the only to Heaven. I choose to believe that his forgiveness doesn't stop at (490) 70 times 7 since, He died for our forgiveness!!! We can't earn forgiveness. It has been paid for already by His blood.

Wolf hunters' food for thought. Since unforgiveness **is unforgivable,** maybe this will help you be able to forgive easier! There once was a man named Saul who persecuted Christians, that when God got his attention, he became Paul. If God had not gotten his attention because of the prayers of Christians, **can you imagine His vengeance** compared to what we could do in our anger, **yes unforgiveness is anger**. God knows what is best! It was very hard to forgive my earthly father until I realized the wrongs were not him but Satin using his weaknesses.

Rom 12:19-20 Beloved do not avenge yourselves, but rather **give place to wrath**; for it is written, "Vengeance is Mine, I will repay," says the Lord. 20 Therefore "If your enemy is hungry, feed him; If he is thirsty, give him a drink; For in so doing, **you** will **heap coals of fire on his head**."

Did we just get a small glance at what hell is like? Coals of fire on someone's head. We should be helping others **as if we could earn eternity with the Messiah, Yeshua, Jesus!** Instead of, reading other books, I felt that the only way I could answer questions about money was to read *the* book—the Bible. I knew I could trust God's Word.

In my early years, I never heard anyone argue about what is in the Old Testament about tithing. It was always "Tithing is not in the

New Testament." We must remember that the Bible works as a whole and never contradicts itself. To refute that idea—that tithing is purely an Old Testament command—I decided that **most of this guide will cover the New Testament's truths about tithing.**

At the start of my Christian walk, I was taught that if you loved the Lord, you tithed. Based on that **something is wrong since only one in ten uses more than their mouth.**

What also drew me to the idea of tithing was something that had me really puzzled: I couldn't understand **why only a few people** had peace when they experienced trials. Some of those people were poor, and others were wealthy. To those few, how little, or how much, they had made no difference. There was a **sense of peace that surrounded them**. It was palpable. **I knew that it was the kind of peace I wanted.**

During my 35 years, I found that my clients, being mostly Christian, who had the peace I wanted, had one thing in common. **They each tithed**! I pray that you will find this the most extensive and comprehensive guide on the subject of Christian money/time, that you have ever read—except for the Word itself.

We must have a good foundation of who we are in Christ. We are all friends and servants. *How many of you would continue to pay a servant who didn't do what you asked?* Let's all look to the future of **how many more that may go home with us by supporting our Christian workers and brothers, as the Messiah, Yeshua, Jesus asked.**

WHERE IS THE CHURCH?

What makes a church? **What about the people** that for many different reasons do not attend a church building or a group meeting?

Webster's dictionary reads, church is the **whole body** of Christian believers.

58% of confessing Christian's in the USA do not go to a building or meeting! Something is wrong!

The % of confessing Christian's has continually gone **down** each of the last 10 years in the USA, while at the **same time the % has gone up each year in China**?!? I am sure it helps that **they aren't given dozens of Christian denominations (religions) to pick from**! We know they tithe closer to 10 out 10 **and** spend way much more time helping each other!

This wolf hunter for Jesus says there is no one in the world because of COVID 19 that doesn't know **there is not one group of any kind that can last without overhead covered** (rent, utilities, worker's pay), Christian's call the tithe (the10%).

***Really think and pray about this! If no time and or money is invested, it means very little to you. We give more attention to something that we put **time** and/or money into so **the more important it becomes.** We are also reminded that everything is His in the first place.

Can You imagine the **growth for God's Kingdom when the first USA leader** (so others may learn what) **really lifts the Messiah,**

Yeshua, Jesus up? Currently only 1 in 10 confessing Christians are sold out 100% believers. There is a way to add to what is being done already, **something we had overlooked**! Out of what **was already there** so that **the other 9 out of 10 will be 100% sold!** After all, they are confessing Christians. The Messiah, Yeshua, Jesus has caught their attention. And what about the 5 of 10 who do nothing? You can't tell me not one had a gain **or** does not, at least, want one reward! Maybe they are mouth only Christian and will hear **depart, I knew you not.**

The **Messiah, Yeshua, Jesus's people are the church**. I pray this **wolf hunter's survival guide** helps.

The last 35 years I have spoken with 1000's of confessing Christians **that are not going to a building or a group meeting**. It seemed to me they read the word more than one's going to a church building or meeting! **God's word equals Heaven. Man's opinions mean nothing,** and too many opinions help people go to hell.

The main reason they brought up was, **why attend a group that thinks a (changed) Bible is, okay?** There are over **25 warnings about changing scripture including some curses**. Which bite, of the perverted word, contains the poison? Buy a new kit. **Why risk the poison and God's wrath?** Be safe, just replace it with KJV that includes Amplified on same page or NKJV. Chapter on warning's coming. **We are talking about heaven or burn in Hell!** See chapter on which survival kit (Bible)later!

They got tired of hearing talks about needing money all the time was next. I have even met people who tithe that left their church because it spent too much time asking for more money. Here is one I heard way too many times, **they sell junk to my grandmother**, as a blessing **to be received, if** she buys this from us.

Since I, myself, one person, has met 1000's, there **must be more than a 100,000,000 in the USA looking for a leader who will stand for full unchanged truth**!

The tithe "is necessary" for the Messiah, Yeshua, Jesus, **from all** our increase. **So, what we are not under the law.** Who should we give it to? They say the big TV and radio ones don't need it.

GOD'S HONOR (your time/money) IS NECESSARY FOR the MESSIAH, YESHUA, JESUS is a chapter coming up. **It will help pull us all together** for the same goal of serving the Messiah, Yeshua, Jesus! It is **so easy it will surprise most of you!**

If you are under someone's teaching, that is where giving the tithe starts. What if their needs are well covered or you feel they have more than they need? Don't let that hold you back! Even if not under someone's teaching, we still want to give God His honor!

When we are helping someone, **if we are doing it for the Messiah, Yeshua, Jesus**, as He asked, our **time**/money **is going directly to part of what the tithes are for in the First Place! That is how the underground churches have grown.**

With COVID-19 maybe we need to follow their examples about helping each other, even giving their lives to help!

The war could stop with our combined prayer, who knows. **We must look long term** by learning more about helping others with **our time/money, since it is God's honor**!

Matt 22:37-40 Jesus said to him, "'You shall love the Lord your God **with all** your heart, **with all** your soul, and **with all** your mind.' 38 This is the first and great commandment. 39 And the second is like it: 'You shall love your neighbor as yourself.' 40 On these two commandments hang all the Law and the Prophets."

Mark 9:39-41But Jesus said, "Do not forbid him, for no one who works a miracle in My name can soon afterward speak evil of Me. 40 **For he who is not against us is on our side**. 41 For whoever **gives you** a cup of water to drink in My name **because you belong to Christ**, assuredly, **I say to you, he will by no means lose his reward.**

Luke 10:3-4 Go your way; behold, I send you out as lambs among wolves.

Matt 10:16 "Behold, I send you out as sheep in the midst of wolves. Therefore, **be wise as serpents and harmless as doves**.

John 8:28-31Then Jesus said to them, "**When** you lift up the Son of Man, **then** you will **know that I am He,** and that I do nothing of Myself; but as **My Father taught Me**, I speak these things.

29 And He who sent Me is with Me. The Father has not left Me alone, **for I always do those things that please Him.**" 30 As He spoke these words, many believed in Him.

*When? **Then**? Less than 1 in 10 honor the Son, **how can we (the body) say we know Him?**

If I had known **how easy real Christianity** is

#1 my, your, our, **time** is God's honor.

#2 God's honor is necessary for His Son the Messiah, Yeshua, Jesus. **So what that**, it's not under law!

#3 that evidence (fruit) accompanies salvation, doesn't earn it.

#4 the tithe can be redeemed, with my **time**, that was exchanged for money to tithe in the first place. No one **would still sit on the side-line knowing they could go to hell** if they knew their **time** can be honor for, the Messiah, Yeshua, Jesus. **So, what I have no increase!**

DO ALL PASTERS/TEACHERS HAVE BLOOD ON THEM

If you have not been taught the full truth about God's honor, your pastor/teacher has blood on them.

It must be serious since Paul cried night and day for 3 years warning everyone. Acts 20:26-31 (the whole counsel, subject) You know who tried to use partial scripture with the Messiah, Yeshua, Jesus.

Since you do love the Messiah, Yeshua, Jesus, you are going to be **blessed out of your socks**. What could be better than **more knowledge** of God's honor?

Partial scripture is very bad and could help send you to hell!

Please remember what a **forgiving and loving God** we serve though His Son the Messiah, Yahshua, Jesus.

As a pastor teacher if you have not taught **each** one of the following you are using partial scripture.

If you have not heard **each** one of the following, please pray for your leader and buy an extra copy of this SURVIVAL GUIDE that you are holding for them.

#1 **your time is** so valuable because it is **God's honor.**

#2 **God's honor is necessary** for His Son the Messiah, Yeshua, Jesus, your best Friend.

#3 The tithe can be redeemed with your **time**, which is (your **time**) replaced with money in the first place!

#4 Where is your evidence(fruit) that accompanies salvation.

#5 The warnings and **curses we are under for not speaking against perverted scripture. Over 25 warnings with some curses!**

Scripture reminds us that **the subject** is hard to explain!

Heb 5:11 of whom we have **much to say**, and **hard to explain**,

Matt 11:29-30 Take My yoke upon you and learn from Me, for I am gentle and lowly in heart, and **you will find rest for your souls**. 30 For My yoke **is easy** and My burden **is light**."

The Messiah, Yeshua, Jesus my best friend, died for all our sins, and only askes that we help others with His honor, my **time**/money so He can honor, His and our, Father. I want the whole world to know!

Yes! True Christianity is that easy!

YOU DECIDE

It is said that 50% of the confessing Christians in the USA don't give anything, that means they have **no evidence (fruit).**

Heb 6:9 But, beloved, **we are confident of better things concerning you,** yes, **things that accompany salvation,**

There may be a few of those 50% that are out helping people like we should. If they're not helping the body that they attend, they are probably not helping.

With no evidence to accompany salvation, **it is no wonder that the Messiah, Yeshua, Jesus is weeping.** He's coming back soon and that means He's going to say to **more than 50%** of the ones who thought they were going home with Him that **they are not welcome! They are going to hell.**

They did not read the word. **No one** told them they must have **evidence that accompanies salvation. Or** that the tithe could be redeemed with our **time** (God's honor). **Or** that it is necessary for God's Son the Messiah, Yahshua, Jesus. **Or** no one told them to read and **not rely on what someone says** unless it matches the word. **It's your life that could pay** with wrong or partial knowledge **not theirs!**

We need the **full truth about how important our time is to God since it is His Honor!**

I said you decide, because if you decide to help teach the full truth about the tithe, making it much easier **for everyone to honor**

the Messiah, Yeshua, Jesus, you will help save some from going to hell!

2 Cor 9:10-12 Now may **He who supplies** seed to the Sower, and bread for food, supply and **multiply** the seed you have sown and **increase** the fruits of your righteousness,11 while you are **enriched in** everything for all liberality, which causes thanksgiving through us to God.12 For the administration of this service not only supplies the needs of the saints, **but also is abounding** through **many thanksgivings to God**,

The wolves main attack signs

This Wolf hunter found that these are the main verses twisted by the wolves, one way or another!

Mal 1:1 The **burden of the word** of the Lord **to Israel** by Malachi.

Mal. 3:9 You are cursed with a curse, for you have robbed Me, **even this whole nation.**

The above two scriptures prove that Malachi was not written just for the priests, **as the wolves lie about**! Do not forget what hurts one in the body hurts all!

Another way to spot a wolf is when **they try to create uncertainty** like about Jacob's tithe in the following verses. Just like Satan with Adam and Eve when he asked, "did He really say?'

Gen 28:15-22 Behold, **I am with you** and will keep you wherever you go and will bring you back to this land; for I will not leave you until I have done what I have spoken to you." Then Jacob awoke from his sleep and said, "Surely the Lord is in this place, and I did not know it." **And he was afraid** and said, "How awesome is this place! This is none other than the house of God, and this is the gate of heaven!" Then Jacob rose early in the morning and took the stone that he had put at his head, set it up as a pillar, and poured oil on top of it. And he called the name of that place Bethel; but the name of that city had been Luz previously. Then Jacob made a vow, saying, "**If God** will be with me, and keep me in this way that I am going, and give me bread to eat and clothing to put on, so that I come back to my father's house in peace, then the Lord shall be my God. And this stone which I have set as a pillar shall be God's house, and **of all** that You give me **I will surely give a tenth to You**."

The wolves try to create doubt with "If God" (Gen 28:20) as if Jacob could ever have uncertainty or doubt in God! **Here** if **means** "since". **Since** God said it, Jacob was so sure about God's word; **he was already building God's house**. Of course, **so what that** he didn't owe the tithe until he received the increase. This is the only thing that is conditional about the tithe—no increase, no tithe. God told him the increase was coming **so he was already building.** Knowing God keeps His word.

By the way, I pray that God will give me an advance notice like that!

Another way the wolves try to create doubt is to say Abraham never tithed or never tithed from his personal belongings. They must have overlooked the following.

Gen. 26:5 Because **Abraham obeyed** My voice and kept My charge, My commandments, My statutes, and My laws.

You have just read the main verses the wolves are using to mislead unknowing Christians. The main way they lie is by rewording or using partial scriptures, **like Satan tried to do with the Messiah, Yeshua, Jesus**!

Partial words create doubt and uncertainty.

Anyone trying to use even one of the above verses to say that tithing is not scriptural today should be shunned.

They are either wolves or have believed a wolf instead of God's non-perverted Word. If anyone disagrees, ask for copy-and-paste, KJV or NKJV, not their opinion. You want what God says, not a man's opinion!

THE TITHE OLD TESTAMENT
set up for New Testament

Mal. 3:1–3 "Behold, I send My messenger, and He will prepare the way before Me. And the Lord, whom you seek, will suddenly come to His temple, even the Messenger of the covenant, in whom you delight. Behold, He is coming," says the Lord of hosts. "But who can endure the day of His coming? And who can stand when He appears? For He is like a refiner's fire and like launderers' soap. He will sit as a refiner and a purifier of silver; He will purify the sons of Levi, and purge them as gold and silver, that they may offer to the Lord an offering in righteousness."

These passages discuss what the Messiah, Yeshua, Jesus will do, and there's no way that He will come back only for the sons of Levi.

Mal. 3:4–6 "Then the offering of Judah and Jerusalem will be pleasant to the Lord, as in the days of old, as in former years. And I will come near you for judgment; I will be a swift witness against sorcerers, against adulterers, against perjurers, against those who exploit wage earners and widows and orphans, and **against those who turn away an alien—because they do not fear Me**," says the Lord of hosts. "For I am the Lord, I do not change; therefore, you are not consumed, O sons of Jacob. Yet from the days of your fathers, you have gone away from My ordinances and have not kept them. **Return to Me, and I will return to you**," says the Lord of hosts. "But you said, '**In what way shall we return?**'"

Mal. 3:4–7 **Will a man rob God**? **Yet you have robbed Me**! But you say, "In what way have we robbed You?" **In tithes and offerings**. You **are cursed with a curse**, for **you have robbed Me**, **even this whole nation.**

Since many Jews do not believe(yet!), that Christ is the Messiah, Yeshua, Malachi's third chapter would be worthless to them. So, was it only written for the Jews of that time and not for the Jews of today and for those of us who are grafted in?

In verse seven, God says we've robbed Him of **His tithes and offerings**. Tithing is a wage owed to the church—a duty.

Romans 4:4 says that for him who works, wages are not counted as grace but as a debt.

Why would anyone expect to be rewarded for paying a debt? Remember, the definition of *tithe* is "a tax for the support of the church (the body)."

Why would God be speaking *only* to the people of that time, as I've heard some say? If that were the case, why not throw out the entire Old Testament? Why did the Holy Spirit make sure it was written down(recorded) for us today?

Mal 3:16 Then those who feared the Lord spoke to one another, And the Lord listened and heard them; So, **a book of remembrance** was written before Him For those who fear the Lord And who meditate on His name.

Mal 3:17-18 "They shall be Mine," says the Lord of hosts, "On the day that I make them My jewels. And I will spare them as a man spares his own son who serves him." 18 Then you shall again discern Between the righteous and the wicked, between one who serves God And one who does not serve Him.

If the wolves were right, that Malachi was written only for the priests, it would appear that the book of remembrance was only for the priests?

What better way to wrap up the Old Testament's last book than with a reference to the coming of the Messiah, Yeshua, Jesus Christ who brings the New Testament, the New covenant.

THE TITHE: NEW TESTAMENT

We, as believers, are in debt to those who do ministry work, and far too many of us are looking for ways to get out of paying our debt. If we are 100% sold out Christian now knowing how valuable our **time** is how can we not at least tithe **time**/money!

Matt 23:23 "Woe to you, scribes and Pharisees, hypocrites! For you pay tithe of mint and anise and cumin and have neglected the weightier matters of the law: justice and mercy and faith. **These you ought to have done**, **without leaving** the others undone.

Some say that He here was talking only to the Scribes and the Pharisees who were under the Mosaic Law and that He used this reasoning so as not to offend them. I believe that being called a hypocrite would offend most people. I cannot believe that there were no Christians in the audience to benefit from hearing also.

Why would His words be included here since He was crucified a short time after He spoke these words if His words do not count anymore after His death and resurrection. He spoke about **taking time** to show justice, mercy and faith.

We don't get to take out the parts of the Scriptures that we don't like and only obey what we do like. You could *try* to take something out, but that does not nullify its truth. You're only hurting yourself when you disobey the Lord.

You will go to hell, if you continue **telling others not to tithe**. Speaking against God's Honor! Where else could you go?

What I'm going to say next will offend some people who believe that the tithe is enough, **which it is**, but **you will be shocked to know the many blessings that can begin after giving of the tithes.** All of you who tithe know this, as you are giving more than the tithe and are being blessed more. To be sure, it is a great blessing here on earth for those who receive the tithe in return for their ministry work. It's a payment—a debt owed for their labor. There are only a few who can afford to work without pay.

Luke 11:42 Jesus also said, "But woe to you Pharisees! For you tithe mint and rue and all manner of herbs and **pass by justice and the love of God**. These you ought to have done, **without** leaving the others undone.

The way we show God our love is by doing what He asks us to do—be obedient. The Messiah, Yeshua, Jesus also spoke this parable (Websters; parable, a short allegorical story (**designed to illustrate or teach religious principle**) to those who were trusting in themselves, thinking they were righteous in tithes while withholding mercy (compassion) to others.

Luke 18:10–14 Two men went up to the temple to pray, one a Pharisee and the other a tax collector. The Pharisee stood and prayed thus with himself, "God, I thank You that I am not like other men—extortioners, unjust, adulterers, or even as this tax collector. I fast twice a week; **I give tithes of all that I possess.**" And the tax collector, standing afar off, would not so much as raise his eyes to heaven, but beat his breast, saying, "God, be merciful to me, a sinner!" I tell you; this man went down to his house justified rather than the other; for everyone who exalts himself will be humbled, and he who humbles himself will be exalted.

The Pharisee in the above parable tried to use tithes to prove that he was righteous. But this does not justify anyone, especially when it is done for attention or for the approval of other men. What God wanted from this Pharisee was his **time—time** to be merciful and enact godly character in his life.

Think about the previous passage considering the old argument: "But tithing is just for Old Testament Jews." If we use this excuse and think that it no longer counts, then we would have to say we can also bypass justice and the love of God. But why would the Messiah, Yeshua, Jesus say, something today that would not mean anything tomorrow? He said that whoever takes **time** to humble himself will be exalted. What a blessing!

Rom 2:22-23 You who say, "Do not commit adultery," do you commit adultery? You who abhor idols, **do you rob temples**?

The tithe is consecrated to God. I've heard some say that this verse doesn't use the word *tithe*, but what else is there in the sanctuary that is consecrated to God that we could rob him of—thereby committing sacrilege?

1 Cor. 16:1–3 Now concerning **the collection for the saints**, as I have given orders to the churches of Galatia, so you must do also: on the first day of the week let each one of you lay something aside, storing up **as he may prosper**, that there be no collections when I come. And when I come, whomever you approve of by your letters I will send to bear your gift to Jerusalem.

Is not the definition of *tithe* "a tenth part of goods or income paid as a tax for the support of the church"? As I thought, support is what the tithe was for! **If the collection was not the tithe**, I guess **we now know that there were two collections—one for support and another one for support**! Well, okay! It's all His anyway!

Are the saints not the leaders and workers in the church? The above verses say that "**you must do also**," but please notice that it also says, "as you may prosper." Paul was talking to the church in Corinth and said that he gave the same order to the churches in Galatia. These were all Christian churches. If you still choose to believe that Paul was not referring to the tithe, you in any case must acknowledge that he did say "a collection for saints on the first day of the week." Why would, the inspired Word of God only be talking to the Christian churches of the past?

2 Cor. 5:14–15 "For the love of Christ compels us, because we judge thus: that if One died for all, then all died; and He died for all, **that those who live should live no longer for themselves**, but for Him who died for them and rose again".

The Issue with Debt

"What if I don't have enough to give my tithe, let alone any offering above? Should I borrow to give to the Lord?" Before I answer that, let's clear up a few things about debt. There's really nothing wrong with using a credit card wisely.

Before I accepted the Lord, I worked as a loan officer; I approved and collected loans. The man who trained me told me to never approve a loan for someone who says they are not worried about how they would pay their loan because the Lord will help them. My worldly trainer thought such a person would become a collection problem or might not even pay.

Since coming to know the Lord, I have heard people say that you should never borrow. If you use one or two scripture verses, you could possibly make that case. When you read all the scriptures about borrowing, you will find that they don't say "Don't borrow." They *do* say that *if* you borrow, you need to be prepared to pay, even as a cosigner, and that it is best not to borrow at all.

Using just a part of the Scriptures pertaining to a particular subject is like having a locale award-winning recipe, and you add an ingredient **that was already there** in the Scripture, **it becomes world winning. Now 10 out of 10 will like it!** The conclusion I have come to, as a money manager, is that if it's done wisely, it's okay. Please be very careful when you use money that the Lord has not yet given to you. **He is not obligated to pay**. If your car is working fine, why would you want to get into debt for a new one? If your television is working, why would you want to borrow money for a new TV?

The savings in interest charges that you can get by paying cash can make a huge difference in your cash flow! Often you get a discount if you pay in cash. I believe too much of advertising is from Satan. It's all about "You deserve this…," "You need this…," or "You must have it, or you won't be happy!" It's all about the *self*, and the *self* is the number-one tool that Satan uses to defeat us: he's been using it since the garden of Eden!

Money used for material goods will never buy true, lasting happiness. However, money and or **time** that is **used biblically can "buy" happiness that is eternal** and provide many blessings while we're here on Earth.

I have also heard some people say that if we don't give, we will not receive. While this statement, itself is true, **please don't get caught up in the "give to get" mentality**, which is another one of Satan's tools. There are people, who are so far in debt that they can't think straight, and you wouldn't want to end up like one of them.

This brings us back to our original question: "Should I go into debt to give offerings to the Lord?"

I know some will argue this point, but I cannot believe **that God would want us to rob** those whom we owe here on earth, **in order, to give to Him**.

Rom. 13:8–10 **Owe no one anything except to love one another**, for he who loves another **has fulfilled the law** For the commandments, "You shall not commit adultery," "You shall not murder," "You shall not steal," "You shall not bear false witness," "You shall not covet," and if there is any other commandment, are all summed up in this saying, namely, "You shall love your neighbor as yourself." Love does no harm to a neighbor; therefore, love is the fulfillment of the law.

In my experience as a loan officer, the man who trained me had a negative opinion about Christians because they often didn't pay their debts. If Christians are so flaky, why would I want to become one?" If you are in debt and you feel you can't give money to the Lord's work, do not forget this:

Rom. 2:4 "Or do you despise the riches of His goodness, forbearance, and long-suffering, not knowing that the goodness of God leads you to repentance?

Ask the Lord to forgive you and to help you develop a plan—in writing and preferably signed and dated. (If you put it in writing, you will not forget that you have made a commitment to the Lord). As He helps you get rid of your debt, plan the amount you will start giving to Him. Then as He helps you get rid of the debt; you can increase your giving. Notice that I said "as He helps you"; this means there must be effort on your part.

I am certain that you'll be surprised by how fast He will help you get out of debt when **your real reason is to help the Messiah, Yeshua, Jesus** and not merely get out of debt. When you honor your commitment, you will not be using all your finances for yourself, as you have in the past. Of course, **in the meantime, use your very valuable time (God's honor) to replace the shortage.**

Who knows? Paying your earthly debt may help bring salvation to that debt collector hounding you. You will also be ministering to the saints—even if it's not the full 10 percent that you owe. **You can redeem with your time.** We serve a very loving and forgiving God.

Giving to help bring others to the Lord so that you can receive more to give **is the only "giving to get" that works**.

When you truly want to be blessed, you must quit using it all for yourself and that **time can replace money**. Remember that you can choose to be a slave to money or be a servant to God.

Luke 16:13 "No servant can serve two **masters; for either he will hate the one and love the other, or else he will be loyal to the one and despise** the other. You cannot serve God and mammon."

How we spend our time determines our reward. Most of us are given money in exchange for our work (of course, some are paid more than others). Money came into existence as a means of barter or exchange. It was easy to trade or barter with one's neighbor, but what if one needed perishable items like food or large items that were impractical to take on a long trip? It was easier to exchange one's work (one's **time**) or one's goods for money, which could then be used to buy needed goods elsewhere.

There have always been different forms of money because anything of value can be used as currency. Salt, gold, silver, precious gemstones, chickens, cows, horses, blankets, clothing, and food are some of the things that are used as money.

All of these are being used as a form of money somewhere in the world today. I'm sure you can think of many other items that are used as a means of barter or exchange. And, again, your **time** has value. "**Time** is money."

I give you my wolf hunter's quote: **The more wisdom and knowledge you have, the more valuable your time is**. **The more valuable your time is, the more money, or the replacement of it, you can earn.** Which means you can help more people, **thereby giving more Honor to God**, thru His Son the Messiah, Yeshua, Jesus.

If I were a betting man, I believe it would be impossible to lose this bet. I would bet there is not one day that goes by in which you don't think about money **in one way or another**. I would even go so far as to say that some of us think more about money during the day than we do about the Lord.

Guess what? **You will receive the blessings or the curses** that have been earned by your use of the time and/or money that has been entrusted to your stewardship. It's your choice. But I'm sure you want blessings. I hope you can't wait to get to the section that discusses the 70 biblical rewards for use of **time** and/or money.

This must be why so much of the Scriptures talks about money and **time**, the use of them. In fact, it is the second-most talked-about subject in the New Testament—especially when you consider time and talent to be equal to money or a replacement for it. For those of you who have fallen on hard times, or out of work, or have fallen so far into debt that your creditors are bugging you, don't forget,

Romans 2:4 says: "Or do you despise the riches of His goodness, forbearance, and long-suffering, not knowing that the goodness of God leads you to repentance? This means that you can forget the past and look toward the future!

The use of your time and talent to help others is the only way to help bring more souls into His kingdom.,

Did you really give enough of your **time** and/or money to replace what was owed on those first fruits?

Leviticus 27:31 says, "If a man **wants at all to redeem any** of his tithes, he shall add one-fifth to it. This tells us that you need to add 20 percent to redeem the tithe.

Let's say that you're blessed with a forty-hour work- week. One-tenth of that, is four hours. Four hours multiplied by sixty minutes equals 240 minutes.

Twenty percent of 240 minutes is forty-eight minutes. So instead of just owing four hours, you need to spend 288 minutes to redeem your tithe. Which if done daily is only 48 minutes for each of 6 days. **Less than 5 hours a week!**

I hope that this helps those who are in debt to realize that there is hope. And don't forget whom the tithe, your **time**/money, blesses— your Lord and Savior, the Messiah, Yeshua, Jesus **and through Him** to His/our Father, God.

If you have **no increase**, there is nothing to tithe from! **You still have your time (God's honor)** that can **earn you over 70 different blessings**. Please see those chapters later.

Let's say, at this time, you're only able to give 5 percent of your increase; then you would only owe 144 minutes to make up for the other 5 percent with your time.

By the way, breaking 144 minutes down to a manageable time equals twenty-four minutes a day for each of six days. Less than half an hour a day! Less than 3 hours a week!

If you are not helping others in some way, you will bring a curse upon yourself because you're not using your time as a proper steward for God.

If you use it for yourself, how can you look forward to receiving a blessing? As I said before, don't forget what a loving, **forgiving** God we serve, and **never give up on trying** to bless the Messiah, Yeshua, Jesus. Your tithe is part of your total giving. It's a starting point, the cornerstone—**a debt you owe**. Failing to pay your tithe is like running red lights. You may be okay for a while, but sooner or later, you will pay for running those red lights!

The more you rob God of your tithes and gifts, the greater the chance you have of bringing a curse upon yourself. Not receiving a blessing is a curse!

Think about it. I'll say it again: Wouldn't it be a curse *to not* receive a blessing promised by God, as a reward for doing something He has asked you to do? And if you don't do what He has asked you to do, why should He reward you?

Please give some thought to this. If the Lord has your money, He probably has the rest of you as well, and that can only bring a blessing. Also remember that we are talking about earning blessings here—not earning eternal life.

Let this be clear: You cannot buy or work your way into heaven!

The **full price for our sin debt has already been paid by the Messiah, Yeshua, Christ Jesus.**

Putting the tithe first helps remind us of who we are living for. Those who are blessed with work look forward to being paid. Work usually takes up most of our day, but if we keep thinking about who we are working for, it keeps us more focused on the Lord throughout that time.

<u>Never give up—no matter how many times you might fail.</u> <u>If you give up, you're showing that you don't have faith in the Messiah, Yeshua, Jesus. The harder you work for something, the more you will appreciate it.</u>

It's time to get real. If you're not at least trying to tithe or do extra work with the 20 percent added, you don't believe what the Word of God says and may not really love the Messiah, Yeshua, Jesus.

Set a good, strong foundation for the use of money. You will surely be blessed, as the Word says. Let's all be good stewards so that more money can go into the Lord's work of helping others.

The best way to help others, is to bring the message of salvation through the Messiah, Yeshua, Christ Jesus to the lost.

<u>Yes, you need to feed and clothe them so that they feel your unconditional love, which will become a reflection of Him in you. That way, they will be more open to your reason for helping them. This is an excellent way to use our **time** and money to serve the Lord.</u>

Heb. 13:20–21 Now may the God of peace who brought up our Lord Jesus from the dead, that great Shepherd of the sheep, working in you what is well pleasing in His sight, through Jesus Christ, to whom be glory forever and ever. Amen.

<u>Gal. 6:9–10 And let us not grow weary while doing good, for in due season we shall reap **if** we do not lose heart. Therefore, as we have opportunity, let us do good to all, especially to those who are of the household of faith.</u>

What about 666?

In this modern age of technology, there's a lot of talk about chip readers and the possibility of getting chips implanted in our hands or someplace else. Christians who've read the book of Revelation tend to get uncomfortable with this because it sounds so much like the mark of the beast (666)! I have been asked about the mark of the beast more than most—probably because of my work with money. The book of Revelation tells us the following:

Rev 13:15-17 He was granted power to give breath to the image of the beast, that the image of the beast should both speak and **cause as many as would not worship the image of the beast to be killed**.

16 He causes all, both small and great, rich and poor, free and slave, to receive a mark on their right hand or on their foreheads, and that no one may buy or sell except one who has the mark or the name of the beast, or the number of his name. Here is wisdom. Let him who has understanding calculate the number of the beast, for it is the number of a man: His number is 666.

Let's zero in on the Word that says if you *don't* worship the beast, you will be killed. Why would the Word say this unless there are some people who will be killed? The only one who will have the courage to stand up to the beast will be a true Christian. A true Christian is *always* willing to die for Christ at any time.

Many Christians are concerned that they may have unknowingly taken the mark of the beast. We serve a loving God. If you're truly worshipping Jesus, how could you be tricked into worshipping the beast?

What if you did somehow *accidentally* receive the mark of the beast (something that I still believe is not possible)? That would be great! Now you'd be able to buy and sell, and you'd be in a position to help others who refused to worship the beast. We must remember that it's not the mark that condemns us; it's the worship of the beast. There is no way you could get the mark without first worshipping the beast, and you cannot worship the beast unknowingly.

Just like the conscious decision you made to accept the Messiah, Yeshua, Jesus Christ, you would have to consciously decide to worship the beast and receive the mark.

So, we give 666 no more thought!

Can a Christian Be Wealthy?

Over the years, I have had many people ask me if it's possible to be a wealthy Christian. Their questions aren't unfounded, especially when you consider verses like these:

"Then Jesus said to his disciples, 'Assuredly, I say to you that it is hard for a rich man to enter the kingdom of heaven. And again, I say to you, it is easier for a camel to go through the eye of a needle than for a rich man to enter the kingdom of God'" (Matt. 19:23–24).

But wait! If you stop there, you'll surely think that a wealthy person can't possibly be a Christian! That's why we must keep the **unchanged** scripture in context. Look at the rest of the passage:

"When His disciples heard it, they were greatly astonished, saying, 'Who then can be saved?' But Jesus looked at them and said to them, 'With men this is impossible, but **with God all things are possible**'" (Matt. 19:25–26).

Yes, a person can be wealthy and a Christian! Let's look at people in the Bible that God's Word says or implies were wealthy.

Matthew 27:57 describes Joseph of Arimathea as rich and a disciple of Jesus in Luke 8:3, we learn of Joanna, the wife of Chuza, "Herod's steward, and Susanna, and many others who provided for Him from their substance.". Joanna would've been considered wealthy as she was the wife of Herod's steward. I hope you find this as interesting as I did when I thought about this Herod is a relative of the one who tried to kill the Messiah, Yeshua, Jesus when He was younger, and he slaughtered so many children in that effort to kill Him. Yet here, in a roundabout way, his relative is helping to provide for His needs.

I hope this encourages those of you who are working for supervisors you're not comfortable with. Compare the rich young ruler to Zacchaeus!

Luke 18:18-23 Now a certain ruler asked Him, saying, "Good Teacher, what shall I do to inherit eternal life?" So, Jesus said to him, "Why do you call Me good? No one is good but One, that is, God. You know the commandments: 'Do not commit adultery,' 'Do not murder,' 'Do not steal,' 'Do not bear false witness,' 'Honor your father and your mother.'" And he said, "All these things I have kept from my youth." So, when Jesus heard these things, He said to him, "You still lack one thing. Sell all that you have and distribute to the poor, and you will have treasure in heaven; and come, follow Me." But when he heard this, he became very sorrowful, for he was very rich.

Here, it's obvious that wealth possessed this ruler. It was his wealth that kept him from following Christ, his love and trust was in his wealth.

Luke 19:2-10 Now behold, there was a man named Zacchaeus who was a chief tax collector, and he was rich. 3 And he sought **to see who Jesus was**, but could not because of the crowd, for he was of short stature. 4 So **he ran ahead and climbed up into a sycamore tree to see Him**, for He was going to pass that way.5 And when Jesus came to the place, He looked up and saw him, and said to him, "Zacchaeus, make haste and come down, for today I must stay at your house."6 So he made haste and came down and received Him joyfully. 7 But when they saw it, they all complained, saying, "He has gone to be a guest with a man who is a sinner." 8 Then Zacchaeus stood and said to the Lord, "Look, Lord, **I give half of my goods to the poor; and if I have taken anything from anyone by false accusation, I restore fourfold.**" 9 And Jesus said to him, "Today **salvation has come to this house**, because he also is a son of Abraham; 10 for the Son of Man has come to seek and to save that which was lost."

Zacchaeus wanted to see the Messiah, Yeshua, Jesus so much that he ran and climbed up a tree and his life was blessed from the resulting encounter. But how did he know that the wealth wasn't his since he had only just received Him, he didn't even have to be asked. It's obvious that wealth did not possess him, like it did the rich ruler. Also, since Zacchaeus had wealth and was a chief tax collector, he probably didn't lack wisdom so I'm going state that he never knowingly cheated anyone out of anything.

Why would he be so bold as to say he would restore four times as much if he knew he had cheated someone? Yes, there are some good Tax Collectors.

Look at Mary, the mother of John Mark.

Acts 12:12 - 14 so, when he had considered this, he came to the house of Mary, the mother of John whose surname was Mark, where many were gathered together praying. 13 and as Peter knocked at the door of the gate, a girl named Rhoda came to answer.

Mary would have been considered wealthy because she had a big house enough to have a large number of people assembled there, as well as a maid. Other Bible versions refer to Rhoda as a servant.

Acts 16 :14-15 Now a certain woman named Lydia heard us. She was a seller of purple from the city of Thyatira, who worshiped God. The Lord opened her heart to heed the things spoken by Paul.15 and when she and her husband were baptized, she begged us comment saying, if you have judged me to be faithful to the Lord come to my house and stay. So, she persuaded us.

Lydia was a dealer in Fabrics. As a businesswoman, she was a good Steward since she worshiped God and had a privilege of the Messiah, Yeshua, Jesus staying at her house.

There are many examples of wealthy Christians in God's word! We need to remember that everything we have belongs to the Lord. We're merely stewards of His grace and benevolence. We are to put our trust in God alone.

When you're wealthy, it's very easy to think you have need of nothing, but in fact, everything we have belongs to the Lord. Your wealth is to be used to help others, as the Lord would want you to do. Those who are wealthy believe they can get or make anything they need, but we are to put our trust in God alone.

Let's look at what the Bible says about wealth specifically:

1 Tim. 6:9–11 But those who desire to be rich fall into temptation and a snare, and into many foolish and harmful lusts which drown men in destruction and perdition. For the love of money is a root of all kinds of evil, for which **some have strayed from the faith in their greediness** and pierced themselves through with many sorrows. But you, O man of God, flee these things and pursue righteousness, godliness, faith, love, patience, gentleness.

1 Tim. 6:17–19 Command those who are rich in this present age not to be haughty, nor to trust in uncertain riches but in the living God, who gives us richly all things to enjoy. **Let them do good, that they be rich in good works, ready to give, willing to share, storing up for themselves a good foundation for the time to come, that they may lay hold on eternal life.**

The Word doesn't say that you should give away all your money and be poor; it says you should use it wisely. You can be spiritually rich if your money is used biblically.

James 2:5-11 Listen, my beloved brethren: **Has God not chosen the poor of this world to be rich in faith and heirs of the kingdom** which He promised to those who love Him? 6 **But you have dishonored the poor man**. Do not, the rich oppress you and drag you into the courts? 7 Do they not blaspheme that noble name by which you are called? 8 **If you really fulfill the royal law according to the Scripture, "You shall love your neighbor as yourself," you do well;** 9 but if you show partiality, you commit sin, and are convicted by the law as transgressors. 10 For whoever shall keep the whole law, and **yet stumble in one point, he is guilty of all.**

Rev 3:15-17 "I know your works, that you are neither cold nor hot. I could wish you were cold or hot. 16 So then, because you are luke-warm, and neither cold nor hot, I will vomit you out of My mouth.17

Because you say, 'I am rich, have become wealthy, and have need of nothing' — and do not know that you are wretched, miserable, poor, blind, and naked —

If you don't use money biblically, ***ouch!*** What God allows us to have, He expects us to use for His kingdom with His leading and wisdom— whether we be rich or poor.

70 Rewards, short form

Starting in Matthew working through Revelation, see later chapters for full scripture.

#1 that you may be sons of your father in heaven.

#2 you shall be perfect.

#3 your Father Himself, will reward you openly.

#4 protection for your heart

#5 food, drink, and clothing will be added.

#6 enter the kingdom of heaven.

#7 considered a wise man.

#8 founded on the rock.

#9 receive healing.

#10 had demons cast out.

#11 disease is cured.

#12 household considered worthy.

#13 peace comes upon your household.

#14 be considered worthy of Jesus.

#15 find your life.

#16 receive God.

#17 receive a prophet's reward.

#18 receive a righteous man's reward.

#19 rest for your soul.

#20 receive return for your investment in Him.

#21 have treasure in heaven.

#22 inherit eternal life.

#23 be called a good and faithful servant.

#24 enter into the joy of the Lord.

#25 have abundance.

#26 you are blessed of God.

#27 serving God.

#28 have a memorial.

#29 all things are clean to you.

#30 received the key of knowledge.

#31 give God pleasure.

#32 you shall be repaid.

#33 receive true riches.

#34 receive your own.

#35 salvation for your household.

#36 be raised from the dead.

#37 help any believe in the Lord.

#38 receive instruction from a holy angel.

#39 remembered in the sight of God.

#40 have the Holy Spirit fall on those around you.

#41 bigger blessing

#42 receive the grace of God.

#43 abundance of joy

#44 an advantage

#45 sufficiency for all things

#46 increase fruits of your righteousness

#47 many thanksgivings to God

#48 others pray for you.

#49 have exceeding grace of God in you.

#50 receive the prize of the upward call of God.

#51 not be unfruitful.

#52 God is well pleased.

#53 blessed in what he does.

#54 your faith made perfect.

#55 be called the friend of God.

#56 be justified by works.

#57 know love.

#58 know you are of the truth.

#59 Assure your heart before God.

#60 have confidence toward God.

#61 whatever we ask, we receive from God.

#62 we abide in God.

#63 God abides in us.

#64 Give God no greater joy.

#65 give witness of your love before the church.

#66 you do well.

#67 you are of God.

#68 God rewards you.

#69 have right to the tree of life.

#70 enter through the gates into the city.

Seventy Biblical Rewards with scripture

For your, **time**/money, (God's honor). Your evidence that accompanies salvation!

Rewards 1-6

Someone once asked me, "If it's not God's, then whose is it?" He added, "If we don't give to God's work, Satan will get it, and he'll take much more than what God is asking for. "God blesses when we give as He has asked us to. To help you track these rewards in your own Bible, I started in Matthew and worked my way through Revelation. Reminder, I copied and pasted NKJV. **Let's look now at the rewards we get** for following God's Word in our lives.

You have heard that it was said, "You shall love your neighbor and hate your enemy." But I say to you, love your enemies, bless those who curse you, do good to those who hate you, and pray for those who spitefully use you and persecute you, that you may be **sons of your Father** in heaven [**Reward #1**]; for He makes His sun rise on the evil and on the good, and sends rain on the just and on the unjust. For if you love those who love you, what reward have you? Do not even the tax collectors do the same? And if you greet your brethren only, what do you do more than others? Do not even the tax collectors do so? Therefore, **you shall be perfect** [**Reward #2**], just as your Father in heaven is perfect. (Matt. 5:43–48; Luke 6:30–36)

When we use our **time** to love, pray for, and do good to our enemies, the blessing is that we are confirming our relationship with the Father. His own Son endured so much on His journey to the grave; how much less should we be like Christ? And as Christ rose from the grave, victorious over sin and death. With Him, so shall you!

Did you notice that through the correct use of your **time**/money, you can reach perfection? Wow, what a blessing! The word *perfection* in this verse means "completion" or "moral uprightness." God wants us to be complete and morally upright in Him. Remember, David referred to this "perfection": "Mark the perfect man and behold the upright: for the end of that man is peace" (Ps. 37:37, KJV).

This perfection doesn't mean you'll never fail; it means that you have achieved everything that God wants from you in that moment. We should strive to live every moment for Him! The only thing that could stop us from achieving completeness is the number-one tool that Satan uses: the *self*.

Think about it: When it comes to sharing, our **time**/money it seems to be the hardest areas for us to acknowledge that we are just God's stewards. If you boil down your resistance to tithing, giving, and serving, you'll discover your own self-interest, self-ownership, and lack of *true* stewardship. We own nothing!

With the correct use of money/**time**, we can get rid of self-interest— Satan's number-one tool against us. If the Lord has our money, He almost assuredly has the rest of us. Some people resist the idea of *selflessness*; after all, if one is taking care of their body, aren't they also only taking care of themselves? No! It's not *our* bodies.

If we are truly the Lord's, we're merely the stewards of our bodies. Therefore, taking care of your body is not an act of self-interest. You are taking care of His property. It *would* be self-interest if all your **time** and money were spent on taking care of your body for a vain reason or in an obsessive way that does not help others. When we have **time**/money invested in helping others, we tend to care for others **and** have a healthy sense of ourselves. **Plus, it helps us to think about the Messiah, Yeshua, Jesus more, since we are doing it for Him.**

Take heed that you do not do your charitable deeds before men, **to be seen by them. Otherwise, you have no reward** from your Father in heaven. Therefore, when you do a charitable deed, do not sound a trumpet before you as the hypocrites do in the synagogues and in the streets, that they may have glory from men. Assuredly, I say to you, they have their reward. But when you do a charitable deed, do not let your left hand know what your right hand is doing, that your charitable deed may be in secret; and your Father who sees in secret **will Himself reward you openly [Reward #3]**. (Matt. 6:1–4)

A charitable deed is an act of kindness that is done to help others while seeking nothing in return, and it, of course, takes **time**/money. I look back at times when I helped others and was disappointed because I didn't get a thank-you.

When I can now, I try to find ways to help others anonymously. Then it doesn't bother me if I'm not thanked; I really like having my heavenly Father reward me!

Do not lay up for yourselves treasures on earth, where moth and rust destroy and where thieves break in and steal; but lay up for yourselves treasures in heaven, where neither moth nor rust destroys and where thieves do not break in and steal. **For where your treasure is, there your heart will be also [Reward #4]**. (Matt. 6:19–21; also, Luke 12:33–34)

Can you imagine the protection our hearts could receive if we were to store our treasures in heaven? Why can't it be our real heart!

My heart It is one of the treasures that God gave me. About 18 years ago, I had a triple bypass. I was going to work on a Wednesday morning, and before I arrived at my office, I had a pain in the top of my chest, underneath my chin. It wasn't a location that I had ever heard of that could be an indication of a heart problem.

I look back now and believe it was the Holy Spirit who prompted me to go into the emergency room.

When I walked in, the nurse asked me what was wrong, and I pointed to where the pain was. She said it probably wasn't anything serious.

When she took hold of my arm to take my blood pressure, she asked if my skin was normally clammy, and as soon as I said no, she decided to do some testing.

Within three or four hours, they knew there was something wrong: One of my veins was 100 percent blocked. Another was 85-95 percent blocked, and a third was 35-40 percent blocked.

It was serious enough that they sent me by ambulance to a different hospital that afternoon, where they scheduled a triple bypass for Friday morning.

Now, before you ask how God was protecting my heart, I want to tell you that there was no heart attack or stroke, damage, that sent me to the hospital. From what I understand, it is quite common to find a vein problem **after damage** from heart attack or stroke.

Therefore, do not worry, saying, "What shall we **eat**?" or "What shall we **drink**?" or "What shall we **wear**?" For after all these things the Gentiles seek. For your heavenly Father knows that you need all these things. But seek first the kingdom of God and His righteousness, **all these things shall be added to you** [Reward #5]. (Matt 6:31–33, also Matt. 10:9–10)

Wow, what a blessing reward # 5 is! Seeking the kingdom of God involves worship and ministry, and ministry always involves either **time**/money—or both. Remember that the **time** spent on work is as valuable as money. So again, **time** is money. Even if we are not paid in money, we are paid with a replacement of it.

Some of my ancestors even used beads, blankets, and horses when they made exchanges. You will find somewhere in the world they are still used as money. To them, they are the same as money.

So, whether you spend **time** or money, you are learning to trust the Lord more and grow His kingdom.

Not everyone who says to Me, "Lord, Lord," shall **enter the kingdom of heaven [Reward #6], but he who does the will of My Father in heaven**. (Matt. 7:21)

And of course, "the will of the Father" is that we first accept His grace and forgiveness for our salvation and then spread the gospel and serve others. **The importance of the above passage should not be overlooked. There are people who think they will enter the kingdom of heaven but will not**, as this passage clearly states. Please pray for discernment to be able to judge yourself. Have you accepted the Messiah, Yeshua, Jesus Christ's atonement for your sins? **Are you doing the will of the Father?**

Rewards 7-16

Therefore, whoever hears these sayings of Mine, **and does them, I will liken him to a wise man [Reward #7]** who built his house on the rock: and the rain descended, the floods came, and the winds blew and beat on that house; and it did not fall, for it was **founded on the rock [Reward #8]**. (Matt. 7:24–25, also Luke 6:46–49)

Is there anyone who doesn't want the Messiah, Yeshua, Jesus to consider them wise? I surely don't want to be considered a stupid person by Him. And guess what? I don't believe there's any middle ground. You're either a wise man or a foolish one.

A wise man or woman may not know everything but will continually seek knowledge. Building my house upon The Rock (the Messiah, Yeshua, Jesus) has certainly been the best decision I have ever made.

Now when the Messiah, Yeshua, Jesus had come into Peter's house, He saw his wife's mother lying sick with a fever. So, **He touched** her hand, and **the fever left her**. And she arose and served them. When evening had come, they brought to Him many who were demon-possessed. And **He cast out the spirits with a word** and **healed all who were sick [Reward #9]**, that it might be fulfilled which was spoken by Isaiah the prophet, saying: "He Himself took our infirmities and bore our sicknesses." (Matt. 8:14–17; see also Mark 1:29–34 and Luke 4:38–41)

The Messiah, Yeshua, Jesus was welcomed into Peter's house. Mark 1:33 says, "And the whole city was gathered together at the door." If Peter had not received the Messiah, Yeshua, Jesus into his house because his cupboards were bare or because he had something else to do and thought he didn't have time, look at the blessings he would've missed out on. His mother-in-law was healed. Can you imagine how long his house was remembered by the whole city **as the place where the Messiah, Yeshua, Jesus healed many**? How many times do you suppose he was thanked for allowing the people to gather at his door to receive healing? When we invite God into our lives, **the reward is that He does His work through us!**

And when He had called his twelve disciples to Him, **He gave them power** over unclean spirits, **to cast them out [Reward #10]**, and **to heal all kinds of sickness and all kinds of disease [Reward #11]**. (Matt. 10:1)

Again, God uses those who give their lives to Him. **The reward is that He empowers us to further His kingdom.** We don't need to have special gifts or talents because He uses all who come to Him.

Now whatever city or town you enter, inquire who in it is worthy, and stay there till you go out. And when you go into a household, greet it. If the **household is worthy [Reward #12]**, let your **peace come upon it [Reward #13]**. But if it is not worthy, let your peace return to you. And whoever will not receive you nor hear your words, when you depart from that house or city, shake off the dust from your feet. Assuredly, I say to you, it will be more tolerable for the land of Sodom and Gomorrah, in the Day of Judgment, than for that city! (Matt. 10:11–15)

I'm sure there isn't anyone out there who would not want more peace in his or her household. Our household could be considered *worthy* by the Lord if we spend **time**/money to help the workers. And, of course, the disciple's peace is the Lord's peace. I'm sure we all want more of His peace!

Who wouldn't want a disciple to stay in his or her house—one with the power and authority over all demons and who can cure diseases and heal the sick? I want one to stay at my house 24 hours a day, 365 days a year!

And he who does not take his cross and follow after Me is not **worthy of Me** [Reward #14]. He who finds his life will lose it, and he who loses his life for My sake **will find it** [Reward #15]. He who receives you receives Me, and he who receives Me **receives Him who sent Me** [Reward #16]. (Matt. 10:38–40; also Mark 9:41 and Luke 9:48, 14:26–27)

Okay, let's stop right here. There's no sense in going any further. There can be no greater rewards than the ones in verses :14- 16. If this doesn't convince you that spending **time**/money on others is worth it, nothing will. Since the joy of the Lord is my strength, and He said it is more blessed to give than to receive, I want to be in that position where He can continue to give me His blessing.

Rewards 17-22

He who receives a prophet in the name of a prophet shall **receive a prophet's reward** [Reward #17]. And he who receives a righteous man in the name of a righteous man shall **receive a righteous man's reward** [Reward #18]. And whoever gives one of these little ones only a cup of cold water in the name of a disciple, assuredly, I say to you, he shall by no means lose his reward. (Matt. 10:41–42)

When we receive a true prophet, we receive the Messiah, Yeshua, Jesus. We therefore receive the Father, and thereby we receive a prophet's reward, when we receive a righteous man, we receive a righteous man's reward.

Take My yoke upon you and learn from Me, for I am gentle and lowly in heart, and you will find **rest for your souls** [Reward #19]. For My yoke is easy and My burden is light. (Matt. 11:29–30)

His yoke is for us to follow His example of being a servant. We don't want to be lazy servants because we know He wasn't lazy. Rest for our souls? As I look back on my life, I realize that the more trust I had put in the Lord—giving Him the opportunity to prove His love for me (which He desires to do for everyone), the more refreshed I felt.

Think of the rest that you have when you're not worrying. The more trust you put in the Lord, the less you worry. Of course, the hardest thing to turn over to the Lord is our use of money **and time**. I don't know about you, but **the more I'm reminded that it's not *my* life (it's His life), the better I feel**. The only time I worry is when I forget that it's His life. If it's His life, *why* do I need to worry?

The bottom line is that I either trust the Messiah, Yeshua, Jesus, or I don't, especially when it comes to Him supplying my needs. To help remind me of this, every time I open my billfold, I see a note in there that says, **A life lived for others is a life worth living**.

I know there have been many times when I opened my billfold to use my debit or credit card to buy something and that note reminded me to think about whether I really needed that purchase. All too often I didn't need it! Seeing that note helped me spend much less money on myself.

It has been the best budget tool I've ever used. Come to think of it, I don't recall any heavenly rewards for money spent on myself, except for the things that teach me to be a better servant, as the living example, the Messiah, Yeshua, Jesus, showed us.

Therefore, hear the parable of the sower: when anyone hears the word of the kingdom, and does not understand it, then the wicked one comes and snatches away what was sown in his heart. This is he who received seed by the wayside. But he who received the seed on stony places, this is he who hears the word and immediately receives it with joy; yet he has no root in himself but endures only for a while. For when tribulation or persecution arises because of the word, immediately he stumbles. Now he who received seed among the thorns is he who hears the word, and the cares of this world and the deceitfulness of riches choke the word, and he becomes unfruitful. But he who received seed on the good ground is he who hears the word and understands it, **who indeed bears fruit** and produces: **some a hundredfold, some sixty, some thirty [Reward #20]**." (Matt. 13:18–23; also Mark 4:13–20; Luke 8:11–15)

Good ground receives the fertilizer of the Word. The more knowledge and understanding of the Word we have, the stronger our roots are. As a securities and life insurance professional, I would say that ninety-nine out of a hundred people who try to get a return of over two times in a year (let alone thirty times or more on their investment) will lose it all.

But guess what? With the Lord, all things are possible. When you're working for Him, the minimum return could be one hundred times the investment or more!

Remember the young lad who gave his five loaves and two fish to the Lord. We know that when the Lord was looking up to heaven, He was first giving them to God.

The Bible says that Christ took them and fed over five thousand men, plus whatever number of women and children were there. There were twelve full baskets left over.

What if the person who had the bread and fish had decided that he would eat them himself or only share them with his friends?

He might have been able to feed ten to fifteen at the very most instead of the more than five thousand who were fed that day.

Now behold, one came and said to Him, "Good teacher, what good thing shall I do that I may have eternal life?" So, He said to him, "Why do you call Me good? No one is good but One, that is, God. But if you want to enter into life, keep the commandments." He said to Him, "Which ones?" Jesus said, "'You shall not murder,' 'You shall not commit adultery,' 'You shall not steal,' 'You shall not bear false witness,' 'Honor your father and your mother,' and, 'You shall love your neighbor as yourself.'" The young man said to Him, "All these things I have kept from my youth. What do I still lack?" Jesus said to him, **"If you want**

to be perfect [Reward #2 again], go, sell what you have and give to the poor, and **you will have treasure in heaven [Reward #21]**; and come, follow Me." But when the young man heard that saying, he went away sorrowful, for he had great possessions. (Matt. 19:16–22; also Mark 10:17–22 and Luke 18:18–23)

As far as I'm concerned, the rich man in this teaching was really a very poor man. He was only satisfied with earthly pleasures. Try to imagine how much greater the treasures in heaven are. **Did you notice that giving and being perfect are tied together again?**

And everyone who has left houses or brothers or sisters or father or mother or wife or children or lands, for My name's sake, shall receive a hundredfold **[Reward #20 again]**, and **inherit eternal life [Reward #22]**. (Matt. 19:29; also Mark 10:30)

Again, God returns on your investment for Him!

Rewards 23-28

For the kingdom of heaven is like a man traveling to a far country, who called his own servants and delivered his goods to them. And to one he gave five talents, to another two, and to another one, to each according to his own ability. And immediately he went on a journey. Then he who had received the five talents went and traded with them and made another five talents. And like- wise he who had received two gained two more also. But he who had received one went and dug in the ground and hid his lord's money. After a long time, the lord of those servants came and settled accounts with them. So, he who had received five talents came and brought five other talents, saying, "Lord, you delivered to me five talents; look, I have gained five more talents besides them." His lord said to him, **"Well done, good and faithful servant [Reward #23]; you were faithful over a few things, I will make you ruler over many things. Enter into the joy of your lord [Reward #24]."** He also who had received two talents came and said, "Lord, you delivered to me two talents; look, I have gained two more talents besides them." His lord said to him,

"Well done, good and faithful servant [Reward #23 again]; you have been faithful over a few things, I will make you ruler over many things. **Enter into the joy of your lord [Reward #24 again]**." Then he who had received the one talent came and said, "Lord, I knew you to be a hard man, reaping where you have not sown, and gathering where you have not scattered seed. And I was afraid and went and hid your talent in the ground. Look, there you have what is yours." But his lord answered and said to him, "You wicked and lazy servant, you knew that I reap where I have not sown and gather where I have not scattered seed." (Matt. 25:14–26; Luke 19:11–27)

The above scripture shows us that the Lord knows what we are capable of. And even though in the parable, He knew the third servant would not work, He gave him an opportunity anyway. But guess what? Even if we were like the third servant in our past, the Messiah, Yeshua, Jesus is always ready to forgive and offer another chance. Hebrews 13:5 says, "He himself has said, 'I will never leave you nor forsake you.'" The first two servants went to work with what they were given and received a hundredfold return. The third one didn't work, and the Lord called him a wicked and lazy servant. I pray that we will never be called wicked and lazy by the Lord.

For to everyone who has, more will be given, and he will **have abundance [Reward #25]**; but from him who does not have, even what he has will be taken away. (Matt. 25:29)

And He will set the sheep on His right hand, but the goats on the left. Then the King will say to those on His right hand, **"Come, you blessed of My Father [Reward #26]**, **inherit the kingdom [Reward #6 again]** prepared for you from the foundation of the world: for I was hungry and you gave Me food; I was thirsty and you gave Me drink; I was a stranger and you took Me in; I was naked and you clothed Me; I was sick and you visited Me; I was in prison and you came to Me." Then the righteous will answer Him, saying, "Lord, when did we see You hungry and feed You, or thirsty and give You drink? When did we see You a stranger and take You in, or naked and clothe

You? Or when did we see You sick, or in prison, and come to You?" And the King will answer and say to them, "Assuredly, I say to you, inasmuch as you did it to one of the least of these My brethren, **you did it to Me [Reward #27].**" (Matt. 25:33–40)

In the above scripture, we are reminded of how important it is for us to serve others, thereby serving our Father.

And these will go away into everlasting punishment, but **the righteous into eternal life [Reward #6 again].** (Matt. 25:46)

And when the Messiah, Yeshua, Jesus was in Bethany at the house of Simon the leper, a woman came to Him having an alabaster flask of very costly fragrant oil, and she poured it on His head as He sat at the table. But when His disciples saw it, they were indignant, saying, "Why this waste? For this fragrant oil might have been sold for much and given to the poor." But when He was aware of it, He said to them, "Why do you trouble the woman? For she has done a good work for Me. For you have the poor with you always, but Me you do not have always. For in pouring this fragrant oil on My body, she did it for My burial. Assuredly, I say to you, wherever this gospel is preached in the whole world, what this woman has done will also be told **as a memorial to her [Reward #28].**" (Matt. 26:6–13; also Mark 14:3–9; Luke 7:36–50; John 12:1–8)

Wolf hunter's food for thought: It appears to me that it really had not yet sunk into the disciples that He was going to lay his life down for all, yet this woman seemed to know. It reminds me of the saying "The Holy Spirit moves in mysterious ways"—mysterious to us, but, of course, not to the Father.

In Luke 7:1–10, we read of a centurion with a beloved servant who was dying of an unnamed illness. When he heard about the Messiah, Yeshua, Jesus, he sent elders of the Jews to Him, pleading for Him to come heal his servant. The Messiah, Yeshua, Jesus went with them to the centurion's house, but the centurion sent friends to Him, saying, "Lord, do not trouble Yourself, for I am not worthy that You should enter under my roof. Therefore, I did not even think myself worthy to come to You. But say the word, and my servant will be healed. For I also am a man placed under authority, having soldiers under me. And I say to one, 'Go,' and he goes; and to another, 'Come,' and he comes; and to my servant, 'Do this,' and he does it." At these words, the Messiah, Yeshua, Jesus marveled and said to the crowd following Him, "I say to you, I have not found such great faith, not even in Israel!" And immediately the servant was healed!

A centurion was commonly thought to have had a hundred to a thousand men working under him. Can you imagine what it would be like to be a servant to a man who cared so much about you? He was a Roman pleading with the Messiah, Yeshua, Jesus to heal his servant. His friends said the **centurion deserved to have his servant healed because he loved the Jewish nation and had built them a synagogue.**

What a steward he must've been. There probably aren't too many Christians who would build a synagogue. He received a healing (a blessing) for someone who was dear to him, a servant!

This man with earthly authority knew that the Messiah, Yeshua, Jesus's authority was so great that He didn't even have to enter his house to heal his servant. We do know that Christ healed his servant (a blessing).

What a great country this could be if our leaders looked after the people like he did. Leaders, too, are stewards.

Rewards 29-34

Then the Lord said to him, "Now you Pharisees make the outside of the cup and dish clean, but your inward part is full of greed and wickedness. Foolish ones! Did not He who made the outside make the inside also? **But rather give alms of such things as you have**; then **indeed all things are clean to you [Reward #29]**. (Luke 11:39–41)

Woe to you lawyers! For you have **taken away the key of knowledge [Reward #30]**. You did not enter in yourselves, and those who were entering in you hindered.

Alms are acts or deeds of mercy. Like the Pharisees, we all know how to make the outside clean, but sometimes we struggle with the inside. The Word says that all things are clean to us if we commit acts or deeds of mercy. Wow! I don't believe I'm oversimplifying it; you know that the Messiah, Yeshua, Jesus's life was focused on alms (helping others). Is not our goal to become more like Him?

I have read Luke 11:52 many times, and it never truly sank in until now that the key to knowledge is in alms. **By reason of use of your time**! I look back on how many times I asked God for wisdom and knowledge, **not realizing that the key that would give me access to knowledge was in alms**. Websters Dictionary; Alms is giving money, food, or other donations to the poor or needy.

Start helping others, and you will gain knowledge. **Thereby use of your time**!

Do not fear, little flock, for it is **your Father's good pleasure [Reward #31] to give you the kingdom [Reward #6 again]**. Sell what you have and give alms; provide yourselves money bags which do not grow old, a treasure in the heavens that does not fail, where no thief approaches nor moth destroys. For where your treasure is, there your heart will be also. (Luke 12:32–34)

If you possess it (it's yours, not God's), it possesses you, as it did the rich young ruler who could not let go. His self was holding him back.

I look back and remember two things I had, that really had me, **because I had to much pride and joy in their being mine**. I found myself **thinking about them too much.** One was a heavy, solid, eighteen-karat gold necklace. The other was a large, beautiful diamond ring so stunning that people I had not seen in years would ask about it since they did not see me wearing it.

*** I'm not saying you should sell yours!

I justified keeping them much longer than I should have by saying that I could never get what I had paid for them if I sold them. Even though that turned out to be true, I gained so much more when I finally got rid of them. The unspeakable joy that came over me at that time, the release I felt—I'll never get over it. No pun intended, but it really was like a weight coming off me.

You may wonder, "How can I provide for myself if I'm giving things away?" **You may be overlooking your most valuable asset, "your time"** In God's eyes, He sees a steward that He can use. **He gives more when you give more**. Giving is like the power to a car. We know the car can't start unless it has power.

We don't really start receiving until we give, which turns the power on. **If your treasure is in heaven, your heart is there also**. What a blessing! In Matthew 6:19, **the curse is the treasure stored here on earth**. These can be lost and corrupted **and remain here when we die anyway**.

Then He also said to him who invited Him, "When you give a dinner or a supper, do not ask your friends, your brothers, your relatives, nor rich neighbors, lest they also invite you back, and you be repaid. But when you give a feast, invite the poor, the maimed, the lame, the blind. And you will be blessed, because they cannot repay you; for **you shall be repaid [Reward #32]** at the resurrection of the just." (Luke 14:12–14

He who is faithful in the least is faithful also in much; and he who is unjust in what is least is unjust also in much. Therefore, if you have not been faithful in the unrighteous mammon, who will commit to your trust **the true riches [Reward #33]**? And if you have not been faithful in what is another man's, who will give you **what is your own [Reward #34]**? No servant can serve two masters; for either he will hate the one and love the other, or else he will be loyal to the one and despise the other. You cannot serve God and mammon. (Luke 16:10–13)

Even though we can't serve God and mammon, we can, without a shadow of doubt, use mammon to serve God. If you look at it through the world's eyes, you may believe you have very little to give. In God's eyes, if you are a faithful steward, He can trust you with much more (a blessing).

If you are unjust or unfaithful, why would He trust you with true riches? As the Messiah, Yeshua, Jesus said, you can only serve one master. You can serve the self through earthly wealth (mammon), or you can serve God.

Rewards 35-41

Now behold, there was a man named Zacchaeus who was a chief tax collector, and he was rich. And **he sought to see who the Messiah, Yeshua, Jesus was**, but could not because of the crowd, for he was of short stature. So, **he ran ahead and climbed up into a sycamore tree to see Him**, for He was going to pass that way. And when He came to the place, He looked up and saw him, and said to him, "Zacchaeus, make haste and come down, for today I must stay at your house." So, he made haste and came down and received Him joyfully. But when they saw it, they all complained, saying, "He has gone to be a guest with a man who is a sinner." Then Zacchaeus stood and said to the Lord, "Look, Lord, I give half of my goods to the poor; and if I have taken anything from anyone by false accusation, I restore fourfold." And Jesus said to him, "Today **salvation has come to this house [Reward #35]**, because he also is a son of Abraham; for the Son of Man has come to seek and to save that which was lost." (Luke 19:2–10)

Why was the rich young ruler asked to sell all he had, when the chief tax collector, Zacchaeus (Luke 19:8), only gave half of his wealth (plus four times anything he had taken falsely from anyone)?

Think about this: Being a chief tax collector, he wasn't without wisdom or knowledge when he made the statement about giving four times what he had wrongfully taken. I believe he knew he hadn't taken anything by false means (i.e., by saying that someone owed more taxes than he or she really did). Most of us know if we have stolen from someone.

As for the rich young ruler, if he had really kept the Ten Commandments, he would've known he was supposed to help the poor. So, it probably would not have made a difference if he were asked to give just a part of what he had instead of all. His self-interest was too great. His wealth possessed him (a curse).

Yet Zacchaeus, whom the crowd accused of being a sinner, **had not even been asked to give anything**. Through his voluntary action, salvation came to his house. The Amplified Bible says that salvation came **to all** the members of that household (a reward).

At Joppa there was a certain disciple named Tabitha, which is translated Dorcas. This woman was full of good works and charitable deeds which she did. But it happened in those days that she became sick and died. When they had washed her, they laid her in an upper room. And since Lydda was near Joppa, and the disciples had heard that Peter was there, they sent two men to him, imploring him not to delay in coming to them. Then Peter arose and went with them. When he had come, they brought him to the upper room. And all the widows stood by him weeping, showing the tunics and garments which Dorcas had made while she was with them. But Peter put them all out and knelt down and prayed. And turning to the body he said, "Tabitha, arise." And she opened her eyes, and when she saw Peter, she sat up. Then he gave her his hand and lifted her up; and when he had called the saints and widows, **he presented her alive** [Reward #36]. And it became known throughout all Joppa, and **many believed on the Lord** [Reward #37]. (Acts 9:36–42)

Tabitha's work of making tunics and garments for the people around her caused the people to love her so much that they went out of their way (it was approximately a twenty-mile round trip) to implore the apostle Peter to come see her and bring her back to life. The Word says that many believed in the Lord because of her.

And they said, "Cornelius the centurion, a just man, one who fears God and has a good reputation among all the nation of the Jews, **was divinely instructed by a holy angel** [Reward #38] to summon you to his house, and to hear words from you." Then he invited them in and lodged them. On the next day Peter went away with them, and some brethren from Joppa accompanied him. And the following day they entered Caesarea. Now Cornelius was waiting for them and had called together his relatives and close friends. As Peter was coming in, Cornelius met him and fell down at his feet and worshipped him. But Peter lifted him up, saying, "Stand up; I myself am also a man." And as he talked with him, he went in and found many who had come together. Then he said to them, "You know how unlawful it is for a Jewish man to keep company with or go to one of another nation. But God has shown me that I should not call any man common or unclean. Therefore, I came without objection as soon as I was sent for. I ask, then, for what reason have you sent for me?" So, Cornelius said, "Four days ago I was fasting until this hour; and at the ninth hour I prayed in my house, and behold, a man stood before me in bright clothing, and said, 'Cornelius, **your prayer has been heard, and your alms are remembered in the sight of God** [Reward #39]. Send therefore to Joppa and call Simon here, whose surname is Peter. He is lodging in the house of Simon, a tanner, by the sea. When he comes, he will speak to you.' So, I sent to you immediately, and you have done well to come. Now therefore, we are all present before God, to hear all the things commanded you by God." (Acts 10:22–33)

Can you imagine the experience Cornelius had? A man in bright clothing stood before him and told him that **his prayers and alms were remembered in the sight of God**. He knew this was a supernatural experience. This is another great example of what happens when alms are involved.

While Peter was still speaking these words, **the Holy Spirit fell upon all those who heard** [Reward #40] the word. And those of the circumcision who believed were astonished, as many as came with Peter, because the gift of the Holy Spirit had been poured out on the Gentiles also. For they heard them speak with tongues and magnify God. Then Peter answered, "Can anyone forbid water, that these should not be baptized who have received the Holy Spirit just as we have?" And he commanded them to be baptized in the name of the Lord. (Acts 10:44–48)

What joy Cornelius must have felt when his relatives and close friends had the Holy Spirit fall upon them and were baptized in the name of the Lord!

And what joy for Peter also! God really showed him that He shows no partiality. And **it all started because of his use of time/ money.**

So now, brethren, I commend you to God and to the word of His grace, which is able to build you up **and give you an inheritance among all those who are sanctified**. I have coveted no one's silver or gold or apparel. Yes, you yourselves know that these hands have provided for my necessities, and for those who were with me. I have shown you in every way, by laboring like this, that you must support the weak. And remember the words of the Messiah, Yeshua, Lord Jesus, that He said, **"It is more blessed to give than to receive"** [**Reward #41**]. (Acts 20:32–35)

We must support the weak. And even though we are blessed when we receive, we are **more blessed** when we give.

Rewards 42-51

Moreover, brethren, we make known to you the **grace of God bestowed** [**Reward #42**] on the churches of Macedonia: that in a great trial of affliction the **abundance of their joy** [**Reward #43**] and their deep poverty abounded in the riches of their liberality. For I bear witness that according to their ability, yes, and beyond their ability, they were freely willing, imploring us with much urgency that we would receive the gift and the fellowship of the ministering to the saints. And not only as we had hoped, but they first gave themselves to the Lord, and then to us by the will of God. So, we urged Titus, that as he had begun, so he would also complete this grace in you as well. But as you abound in everything, in faith, in speech, in knowledge, in all diligence, and in your love for us—see that you abound in this grace also. I speak not by commandment, but I am testing the sincerity of your love by the diligence of others. For you know the grace of our Messiah, Yeshua,

Lord Jesus Christ, that though He was rich, yet for your sakes He became poor, that you through His poverty might become rich. And in this I give advice: **it is to your advantage [Reward #44]** not only to be doing what you began and were desiring to do a year ago; but now you also must complete the doing of it; that as there was a readiness to desire it, so there also may be a completion out of what you have. **For if there is first a willing mind, it is accepted according to what one has, and not according to what he does not have**. For I do not mean that others should be eased, and you burdened; **but by an equality, that now at this time your abundance may supply their lack, that their abundance also may supply your lack— that there may be equality.** (2 Cor. 8:1–14)

Verse :12 tells us that if there is first a willing mind, it makes no difference how little you may have. Verse :2 says that we can receive joy even in our deep poverty! I believe the reason we can receive joy in our deep poverty is because we are still giving, thereby proving we trust and love the Lord.

But this I say: He who sows sparingly will also reap sparingly, and he who sows bountifully will also reap bountifully. So, let each one give as he purposes in his heart, not grudgingly or of necessity; for God loves a cheerful giver. And God is able to make all grace abound toward you, that you, always having all **sufficiency in all things [Reward #45]**, may have an **abundance for every good work [Reward #26 again]**. As it is written: "He has dispersed abroad, He has given to the poor; His righteousness endures forever." Now may He who supplies seed to the Sower, and bread for food, supply and **multiply the seed you have sown [Reward #20 again]** and **increase the fruits of your righteousness [Reward #46]**, while you are enriched in everything for all liberality, which causes thanksgiving through us to God. For the administration of this service not only supplies the needs of the saints, but also is abounding through **many thanksgivings to God [Reward #47]** while, through the proof of this ministry, they glorify God for the obedience of your confession to the gospel of Christ, and for your liberal sharing with them and all men, and **by their prayer for you** [Reward #48], who long for you because of **the exceeding grace of God in you** [Reward #49]. Thanks be to God for His indescribable gift! (2 Cor. 9:6–15)

When you start giving, you will begin to trust more in the Lord. If you don't give, you're saying that you don't trust the Lord. **Even if you don't have money**, remember that **time is money**, if the **time** is used wisely. Ask your pastor if there is someone who needs help in your church—for example, someone may be ill and need help with mowing their lawn or cleaning their house. If you have a voice, why not smile at the next person you meet and tell them, "Jesus loves you." Can you imagine the blessing the Lord will give you when a person receives Jesus as their Lord because of your small effort? And what if they don't receive the Lord? Your effort will still be rewarded. But sooner or later, someone will respond. If you truly want to be blessed, even when you don't have assets or money to give, you can find a way to **help someone with your time**. Galatians 6:4–5 says, "But **let each one examine his own work**, and then he will have rejoicing in himself alone, and not in another. For each one shall bear his own load." Think about how good you feel when you finish a project that you started, especially if it's something you didn't think you could do. You'll be giving all the glory to the Lord for his helping you!

Not that I have already attained or am already perfected; but I press on, that I may lay hold of that for which Christ Jesus has also laid hold of me. Brethren, I do not count myself to have apprehended; but one thing I do, **forgetting those things which are behind and reaching forward** to those things which are ahead, I press toward the goal for the prize of the **upward call of God** [Reward #50] in Christ Jesus. Therefore, let us, as many as are mature, have this mind; and if in anything you think otherwise, God will reveal even this to you. Nevertheless, to the degree that we have already attained, let us walk by the same rule, let us be of the same mind. (Phil. 3:12–16)

Even if I tried, I probably couldn't count the number of times that this scripture saved me when Satan reminded me of my past in an effort to defeat me. I know that God *totally* forgets my sin (even if *I* don't forget) because His scripture says so. I do know that I am forgiven.

And let our people also learn to **maintain good works**, to meet urgent needs, **that they may not be unfruitful [Reward #51]**. (Titus 3:14)

Rewards 52- 70

But do not forget to **do good and to share**, for with such sacrifices **God is well pleased [Reward #52]**. (Heb. 13:16)

But be doers of the word, and **not hearers only, deceiving yourselves**. For if anyone is a hearer of the word and not a doer, he is like a man observing his natural face in a mirror; for he observes himself, goes away, and immediately forgets what kind of man he was. But he who looks into the perfect law of liberty and continues in it and **is not a forgetful hearer but a doer of the work**, this one will be **blessed in what he does [Reward #53]**. If anyone among you thinks he is religious and does not bridle his tongue but deceives his own heart, this one's religion is useless. Pure and undefiled religion before God and the Father is this: to visit orphans and widows in their trouble, and to keep oneself unspotted from the world. (James 1:22–27)

Remember, the Scriptures say **we are to help those who cannot return the favor**; if we do so, God will openly reward us.

So, speak and so do as those who will be judged by the law of liberty. For judgment is without mercy to the one who has shown no mercy. Mercy triumphs over judgment. What does it profit, my brethren, if someone says he has faith but does not have works? Can faith save him? If a brother or sister is naked and destitute of daily food, and one of you says to them, "Depart in peace, be warmed and filled," but you do not give them the things which are needed for the body, what does it profit? Thus, also faith by itself, if it does not have works, is dead. But someone will say, "You have faith, and I have works." Show me your faith without your works, and I will show you my faith by my works. You believe that there is one God. You do well. Even the demons believe—and tremble! But do you want to know, O foolish man, that faith without works is dead? Was not Abraham our father justified by works when he offered Isaac his son on the altar? Do you see that **faith was working together with his works**, and **by works faith was made perfect** [Reward #54]? And the Scripture was fulfilled which says, "Abraham believed God, and it was accounted to him for righteousness." And he was **called the friend of God** [Reward #55]. You see then that **a man is justified by works** [Reward #56], and **not by faith only**. Likewise, was not Rahab the harlot also justified by works when she received the messengers and sent them out another way? For as the body without the spirit is dead, so faith without works is dead also. (James 2:12–26)

I think it's easy to understand that Abraham was justified by works, but so was Rahab the harlot. This is amazing and should give us all hope in our works. **We're no better than Rahab**, but faith was given to her **so that** she could **do good works**. Verse :22 says that by works, faith is made perfect (i.e., complete).

By this we **know love** [Reward #57], because He laid down His life for us. And we also ought to lay down our lives for the brethren. But who- ever has this world's goods, and sees his brother in need, and shuts up his heart from him, how does the love of God abide in him? My little children, let us not love in word or with tongue, but indeed and truth. And by this we **know that we are of the truth** [Reward #58] and shall **assure our hearts before Him** [Reward #59]. For if our heart condemns us, God is greater than our heart, and knows all things. Beloved, if our heart does not condemn us, we **have confidence toward God**. [Reward #60]. And **whatever we ask, we receive from Him** [Reward #61] because we keep His commandments and do those things that are **pleasing in His sight** [Reward #52 again]. And this is His commandment: that we should believe on the name of His Son

Jesus Christ and love one another, as He gave us commandment. Now he who keeps His commandments **abides in Him** [**Reward #62**], and **He in him** [**Reward #63**]. And by this we know that He abides in us, by the Spirit whom He has given us. (1 John 3:16–24)

If we want to know or experience love, we need to live for others. Ultimately, I do not believe there is anyone who does not—deep down—want to experience love.

The sooner you start helping others, the sooner you will experience it.

By our work, we assure our hearts before God, and this gives us confidence toward God since we know we're pleasing Him.

Who in their right mind would not want to please God? I can't think of a greater joy than to know that I am pleasing God.

Beloved, I pray that you may prosper in all things and be in health, just as your soul prospers. For I rejoiced greatly when brethren came and **testified of the truth that is in you**, **just as you walk in the truth**. **I have no greater joy** [**Reward #64**] than to hear that my children **walk in truth**. Beloved, you do faithfully whatever you do for the brethren and for strangers, who have borne **witness of your love before the church** [**Reward #65**]. If you send them forward on their journey in a manner worthy of God, **you will do well** [**Reward #66**], because they went forth for His name's sake, taking nothing from the Gentiles.

We therefore ought to receive such, that we may become fellow workers for the truth. I wrote to the church, but Diotrephes, who loves to have the preeminence among them, does not receive us. Therefore, if I come, I will call to mind his deeds which he does, prating against us with malicious words. And not content with that, he himself does not receive the brethren, and forbids those who wish to, putting them out of the church. Beloved, do not imitate what is evil, but what is good. He **who does good is of God** [**Reward #67**], but he who does evil has not seen God. (3 John 2–11)

"And behold, I am coming quickly, and **My reward is with Me [Reward #68]** to give to everyone according to his work. I am the Alpha and the Omega, the Beginning and the End, the First and the Last." **Blessed [Reward #27 again]** are those who do His commandments, that they may **have the right to the tree of life [Reward #69], may enter through the gates into the city [Reward #70].** (Rev. 22:12–14)

Talk about **holding the best for last**. Reread #69 & #70. Please help more be able to hear the full truth about God's Honor, so they will not hear depart I knew you not. Remember **it is someone who thinks they are getting in** and **could be one of your children, grandchildren or a friend** who took someone's word instead of reading the right bible. Buy copies of this guide for everyone you know, since it is hard to explain as scripture says, but his yoke is easy, and his burden is light! It is when time is money and money can buy time. **How can God's Honor not be necessary for His Son?**

Each of the above rewards **came after** someone spent time and/ or money helping someone else. I hope you find it as interesting as I have that the last reward listed in the New Testament is that you may enter through the gates into the city. Any Christian reader who has taken the time to get this far will probably never hear Jesus say, "Depart. I knew you not." You would not have taken the time to finish reading this unless you know the loving, forgiving God we serve and trust. That there is still hope for us. **The Scriptures repeatedly remind us to never give up**. May we all trust Him with our time and money so that we can hear, "Well done, good and faithful servant!"

This wolf hunter for Jesus will close with. There is no one in the world because of COVID 19 that doesn't know there is not one group of any kind that can last without overhead covered (employee's, worker's pay). Way too many businesses have gone under, damaging millions of families.

2 Cor 9:10-12 Now may **He who supplies** seed to the Sower, and bread for food, supply and **multiply** the **seed you have sown and increase** the fruits of your righteousness, 11 while you are **enriched in** everything for all liberality, which causes thanksgiving through us to God. 12 For the administration of this service not only supplies the needs of the saints, **but also is abounding through many thanksgivings to God,**

70 PROPHECIES, short form.

<u>**Copy this short form to help win souls**</u>. The scripture is at end <u>of this Guide.</u>

I have been told the Messiah, Yeshua, Jesus fulfilled over 100 prophecies!

<u>**Over 1000 years**, 5 different Jewish prophets gave over 100 different prophecies, the first ones by Moses. **All are** written down, **as recorded evidence** in the Torah which is **the same recorded evidence** in the first five books of our Christian Old Testament. I have only listed about 70+.</u>

<u>**500 years later all were fulfilled!!! Based on the recorded evidence, it's impossible that the Messiah, Yeshua, Jesus is not "The Son of God".**</u>

#1 I will put enmity between.

#2 will bruise Satan's head.

#3 all families and nations blessed through Abraham's seed.

#4 I will establish my covenant with Abraham.

#5 be from the seed of Isaac.

#6 being from the seed of Judah.

#7 have no broken bones.

#8 consecrated to God.

#9 not left overnight on the cross.

#10 be from the seed of Jacob.

#11 be a prophet.

#12 God will establish the throne of his kingdom.

#13 the rulers of the king's counsel together against.

#14 pierce his hands and feet.

#15 soldiers divide garments.

#16 cast lots for his clothing.

#17 false come against.

#18 hated without cause.

#19 do God's will.

#20 love righteousness.

#21 hate, wickedness.

#22 stranger to his own brothers.

#23 zeal for God's house.

#24 given gall for food.

#25 given vinegar for drink.

#26 kings bring presents and gifts.

#27 kings will worship Him.

#28 He will deliver the needy.

#29 will speak in parables.

#30 give himself to prayer.

#31 a priest forever according to the order of Melchizedek.

#32 builders reject.

#33 become chief cornerstone.

#34 people will not hear and see.

#35 virgin's firstborn is a son.

#36 His name Immanuel.

#37. He will be as a sanctuary.

#38 A stone of stumbling.

#39 a rock of offense.

#40 ministry in Zebulun and in the land of Naphtali.

#41 Government will rest on his shoulder.

#42 to order it and establish it with judgment and justice.

#43 be from the stem of Jesse.

#44 spirit of the Lord shall rest upon

#45 deaf shall hear.

#46 blind shall see.

47 will heal the lame.

#48 will heal tongue of the dumb.

#49 voice of one crying in the wilderness.

#50 is like a shepherd.

#51 God will delight him.

#52 be as a light to the Gentiles.

#53 will be whipped.

#54 Beard plucked.

#55 will be spit upon.

#56 as a witness to the people.

#57 will come to Zion.

#58 anointed to preach.

#59 Rachel will weep for her children.

#60 will make a new covenant.

#61 I will be their God; they shall be my people.

#62 of his people.

#63 His name Israel.

#64 come out of Egypt.

#65 will pour out His Spirit.

#66 Jerusalem there shall be deliverance.

#67 who's going forth are from of old, from everlasting.

#68 Whosoever calls on the name of the Lord shall be saved.

#69 will dwell in our midst.

#70 will send Elijah.

70 PROPHECIES WITH SCRIPTURE

I chose not to make any comments in this section. I felt it important they are here even though for most of us the earlier short list is enough!

Genesis 3:14–15: "So the Lord God said to the serpent: 'Because you have done this, you are cursed more than all cattle and more than every beast of the field; On your belly you shall go and you shall eat dust All the days of your life. And I will put enmity between you and the woman and between your seed and her Seed; He shall bruise your head and you shall bruise His heel.'"

Galatians 4:4: "But when the fullness of the time had come, God sent forth His Son, born of a woman, born under the law."

Hebrews 2:14: "Inasmuch then as the children have partaken of flesh and blood, He Himself likewise shared in the same, that through death He might destroy him who had the power of death, that is, the devil."

First John 3:8: "He who sins is of the devil, for the devil has sinned from the beginning. For this purpose, the Son of God was manifested, that He might destroy the works of the devil.

Genesis 12:3: "I will bless those who bless you, And I will curse him who curses you; And in you all the families of the earth shall be blessed.

Genesis 18:17–18: "And the Lord said, 'Shall I hide from Abraham what I am doing, since Abraham shall surely become a great and mighty nation, and all the nations of the earth shall be blessed in him?'"

Genesis 22:18: "In your seed all the nations of the earth shall be blessed, because you have obeyed My voice."

Genesis 26:2–4: "Then the Lord appeared to him and said: 'Do not go down to Egypt; live in the land of which I shall tell you. Dwell in this land, and I will be with you and bless you; for to you and your descendants I give all these lands, and I will perform the oath which I swore to Abraham your father. And I will make your descendants multiply as the stars of heaven; I will give to your descendants all these lands; and in your seed all the nations of the earth shall be blessed.'"

Acts 3:25–26: "You are sons of the prophets, and of the covenant which God made with our fathers, saying to Abraham, 'And in your seed all the families of the earth shall be blessed.' To you first, God, having raised up His Servant Jesus, sent Him to bless you, in turning away every one of you from your iniquities."

Genesis 17:7–8: "And I will establish My covenant between Me and you and your descendants after you in their generations, for an everlasting covenant, to be God to you and your descendants after you. Also, I give to you and your descendants after you the land in which you are a stranger, all the land of Canaan, as an everlasting possession; and I will be their God."

Genesis 21:12: "But God said to Abraham, 'Do not let it be displeasing in your sight because of the lad or because of your bond- woman. Whatever Sarah has said to you, listen to her voice; for in Isaac your seed shall be called.'"

Galatians 3:16: "Now to Abraham and his Seed were the promises made. He does not say, 'And to seeds,' as of many, but as of one, 'And to your Seed,' who is Christ.

Hebrews 2:16: "For indeed He does not give aid to angels, but He does give aid to the seed of Abraham.

Genesis 17:19: "Then God said: 'No, Sarah your wife shall bear you a son, and you shall call his name Isaac; I will establish My covenant with him for an everlasting covenant, and with his descendants after him.'"

Genesis 21:12: "But God said to Abraham, 'Do not let it be displeasing in your sight because of the lad or because of your bond- woman. Whatever Sarah has said to you, listen to her voice; for in Isaac your seed shall be called.'"

Matthew 1:1–2: "The book of the genealogy of Jesus Christ, the Son of David, the Son of Abraham: Abraham begot Isaac, Isaac begot Jacob, and Jacob begot Judah and his brothers."

Romans 9:7: "Nor are they all children because they are the seed of Abraham; but, 'In Isaac your seed shall be called.'"

Hebrews 11:17–19: "By faith Abraham, when he was tested, offered up Isaac, and he who had received the promises offered up his only begotten son, of whom it was said, 'In Isaac your seed shall be called,' concluding that God was able to raise him up, even from the dead, from which he also received him in a figurative sense."

Genesis 49:8–10: "Judah, you are he whom your brothers shall praise; Your hand shall be on the neck of your enemies; Your father's children shall bow down before you. Judah is a lion's whelp; From the prey, my son, you have gone up. He bows down, he lies down as a lion; And as a lion, who shall rouse him? The scepter shall not depart from Judah, nor a lawgiver from between his feet, Until Shiloh comes And to Him shall be the obedience of the people."

Matthew 1:1–3: "The book of the genealogy of Jesus Christ, the Son of David, the Son of Abraham: Abraham begot Isaac, Isaac begot Jacob, and Jacob begot Judah and his brothers. Judah begot Perez and Zerah by Tamar, Perez begot Hezron and Hezron begot Ram."

Hebrews 7:14: "For it is evident that our Lord arose from Judah, of which tribe Moses spoke nothing concerning priesthood."

Revelation 5:5: "But one of the elders said to me, 'Do not weep. Behold, the Lion of the tribe of Judah, the Root of David, has prevailed to open the scroll and to loose its seven seals.'"

Exodus 12:46: "In one house it shall be eaten; you shall not carry any of the flesh outside the house, nor shall you break one of its bones."

John 19:31–36: "Therefore, because it was the Preparation Day, that the bodies should not remain on the cross on the Sabbath (for that Sabbath was a high day), the Jews asked Pilate that their legs might be broken, and that they might be taken away. Then the soldiers came and broke the legs of the first and of the other who was crucified with Him. But when they came to Jesus and saw that He was already dead, they did not break His legs. But one of the soldiers pierced His side with a spear, and immediately blood and water came out. And he who has seen has testified, and his testimony is true; and he knows that he is telling the truth, so that you may believe. For these things were done that the Scripture should be fulfilled, 'Not one of His bones shall be broken.'"

Exodus 13:2: "'Consecrate to Me all the firstborn, whatever opens the womb among the children of Israel, both of man and beast; it is Mine."

Numbers 3:13: "Because all the firstborn are Mine. On the day that I struck all the firstborn in the land of Egypt, I sanctified to Myself all the firstborn in Israel, both man and beast. They shall be Mine: I am the Lord."

Numbers 8:17: "For all the firstborn among the children of Israel are Mine, both man and beast; on the day that I struck all the firstborn in the land of Egypt I sanctified them to Myself."

Luke 2:7: "And she brought forth her firstborn Son, and wrapped Him in swaddling clothes, and laid Him in a manger, because there was no room for them in the inn."

Numbers 9:12: "They shall leave none of it until morning, nor break one of its bones. According to all the ordinances of the Passover they shall keep it.

Deuteronomy 21:23: "His body shall not remain overnight on the tree, but you shall surely bury him that day, so that you do not defile the land which the Lord your God is giving you as an inheritance; for he who is hanged is accursed of God."

Galatians 3:134: "Christ has redeemed us from the curse of the law, having become a curse for us (for it is written, 'Cursed is every- one who hangs on a tree')."

John 19:31–36: "Therefore, because it was the Preparation Day, that the bodies should not remain on the cross on the Sabbath (for that Sabbath was a high day), the Jews asked Pilate that their legs might be broken, and that they might be taken away. Then the soldiers came and broke the legs of the first and of the other who was crucified with Him. But when they came to Jesus and saw that He was already dead, they did not break His legs. But one of the soldiers pierced His side with a spear, and immediately blood and water came out. And he who has seen has testified, and his testimony is true; and he knows that he is telling the truth, so that you may believe. For these things were done that the Scripture should be fulfilled, 'Not one of His bones shall be broken.'"

Numbers 24:17–19: "'I see Him, but not now; I behold Him, but not near; A Star shall come out of Jacob; A Scepter shall rise out of Israel and batter the brow of Moab and destroy all the sons of tumult. And Edom shall be a possession; Seir also, his enemies, shall be a possession, while Israel does valiantly. Out of Jacob One shall have dominion and destroy the remains of the city.'"

Matthew 1:2: "Abraham begot Isaac, Isaac begot Jacob, and Jacob begot Judah and his brothers."

Luke 1:33: "And He will reign over the house of Jacob forever, and of His kingdom there will be no end."

Deuteronomy 18:15: "'The Lord your God will raise up for you a Prophet like me from your midst, from your brethren. Him you shall hear.'"

Deuteronomy 18:18–19: "I will raise up for them a Prophet like you from among their brethren, and will put My words in His mouth, and He shall speak to them all that I command Him. And it shall be that whoever will not hear My words, which He speaks in My name, I will require it of him."

Matthew 21:11: "So the multitudes said, 'This is Jesus, the prophet from Nazareth of Galilee.'"

Luke 7:16: "Then fear came upon all, and they glorified God, saying, 'A great prophet has risen up among us' and, 'God has visited His people.'"

John 6:14: "Then those men, when they had seen the sign that Jesus did, said, 'This is truly the Prophet who is to come into the world.'"

John 7:40 "Therefore many from the crowd, when they heard this saying, said, 'Truly this is the Prophet.'"

Acts 3:18–22: "But those things which God foretold by the mouth of all His prophets, that the Christ would suffer, He has thus fulfilled.

Repent therefore and be converted, that your sins may be blotted out, so that times of refreshing may come from the presence of the Lord, and that He may send Jesus Christ, who was preached to you before, whom heaven must receive until the times of restoration of all things, which God has spoken by the mouth of all His holy prophets since the world began. For Moses truly said to the fathers, 'The Lord your God will raise up for you a Prophet like me from your brethren. Him you shall hear in all things, whatever He says to you.'"

2 Sam 7:12–13: "When your days are fulfilled and you rest with your fathers, I will set up your seed after you, who will come from your body, and I will establish his kingdom. He shall build a house for My name, and I will establish the throne of his kingdom forever.'"

Matthew 1:1: "The book of the genealogy of Jesus Christ, the Son of David, the Son of Abraham."

Psalm 2:1–2: "Why do the nations rage, And the people plot a vain thing? The kings of the earth set themselves, And the rulers take counsel together, Against the Lord and against His Anointed,"

Matthew 12:14: "Then the Pharisees went out and plotted against Him, how they might destroy Him."

Matthew 26:3–4: "Then the chief priests, the scribes, and the elders of the people assembled at the palace of the high priest, who was called Caiaphas, and plotted to take Jesus by trickery and kill Him."

Matthew 26:47: "And while He was still speaking, behold, Judas, one of the twelve, with a great multitude with swords and clubs, came from the chief priests and elders of the people."

Psalm 22:15–16: "My strength is dried up like a potsherd, And My tongue clings to My jaws; You have brought Me to the dust of death. For dogs have surrounded Me; The congregation of the wicked has enclosed Me. They pierced My hands and My feet."

John 20:25–29: "The other disciples therefore said to him, 'we have seen the Lord'. So he said to them, 'Unless I see in His hands the print of the nails, and put my finger into the print of the nails, and put my hand into His side, I will not believe.' And after eight days His disciples were again inside, and Thomas with them. Jesus came, the doors being shut, and stood in the midst, and said, 'Peace to you!' Then He said to Thomas, 'Reach your finger here, and look at My hands; and reach your hand here and put it into My side. Do not be unbelieving but believing.' And Thomas answered and said to Him, 'My Lord and my God!' Jesus said to him, 'Thomas, because you have seen Me, you have believed. Blessed are those who have not seen and yet have believed.'"

Psalm 22:18: "They divide My garments among them, And for My clothing they cast lots."

John 19:23–24: "Then the soldiers, when they had crucified Jesus, took His garments and made four parts, to each soldier a part and also the tunic. Now the tunic was without seam, woven from the top in one piece. They said therefore among themselves, 'Let us not tear it, but cast lots for it, whose it shall be,' that the Scripture might be fulfilled which says, 'They divided My garments among them, And for My clothing they cast lots.' Therefore, the soldiers did these things.

Psalm 27:12: "Do not deliver me to the will of my adversaries; For false witnesses have risen against me and such as breathe out violence."

Psalm 35:11: "Fierce witnesses rise up."

Matthew 26:60: "But found none. Even though many false witnesses came forward, they found none. But at last two false witnesses came forward."

Mark 14:55–61: "Now the chief priests and all the council sought testimony against Jesus to put Him to death but found none. For many bore false witness against Him, but their testimonies did not agree. Then some rose up and bore false witness against Him, saying, 'We heard Him say, "I will destroy this temple made with hands, and within three days I will build another made without hands."' But not even then did their testimony agree. And the high priest stood up in the midst and asked Jesus, saying, 'Do You answer nothing? What is it these men testify against You?' But He kept silent and answered nothing. Again the high priest asked Him, saying to Him, 'Are You the Christ, the Son of the Blessed?'"

Matthew 26:60–61: "But found none. Even though many false witnesses came forward, they found none. But at last two false wit- nesses came forward."

Mark 14:55–59: "Now the chief priests and all the council sought testimony against Jesus to put Him to death, but found none. For many bore false witness against Him, but their testimonies did not agree. Then some rose up and bore false witness against Him, saying, 'We heard Him say, "I will destroy this temple made with hands, and within three days I will build another made without hands."' But not even then did their testimony agree."

Psalm 35:19: "Let them not rejoice over me who are wrongfully my enemies; Nor let them wink with the eye who hate me without a cause."

John 15:24–25: "If I had not done among them the works which no one else did, they would have no sin; but now they have seen and also hated both Me and My Father. But this happened that the word might be fulfilled which is written in their law, 'They hated Me without a cause.'

Psalm 40:7–8: "Then I said, 'Behold, I come; In the scroll of the book it is written of me. I delight to do Your will, O my God, And Your law is within my heart.'"

Matthew 26:39: "He went a little farther and fell on His face, and prayed, saying, 'O My Father, if it is possible, let this cup pass from Me; nevertheless, not as I will, but as You will.'"

Hebrews 10:5–9: "Therefore, when He came into the world, He said: 'Sacrifice and offering You did not desire, but a body You have prepared for Me. In burnt offerings and sacrifices for sin You had no pleasure. Then I said, "Behold, I have come—In the volume of the book it is written of Me—To do Your will, O God."' Previously saying, 'Sacrifice and offering, burnt offerings, and offerings for sin You did not desire, nor had pleasure in them (which are offered according to the law),' then He said, 'Behold, I have come to do Your will, O God.' He takes away the first that He may establish the second."

Psalm 45:6–7: "Your throne, O God, is forever and ever; A scepter of righteousness is the scepter of Your kingdom. You love righteousness and hate wickedness; Therefore God, Your God, has anointed You With the oil of gladness more than Your companions."

Hebrews 1:8–9: "But to the Son He says: 'Your throne, O God, is forever and ever; A scepter of righteousness is the scepter of Your kingdom. You have loved righteousness and hated lawlessness.

Therefore God, Your God, has anointed You With the oil of gladness more than Your companions.'"

Psalm 69:8–9: "I have become a stranger to my brothers, and an alien to my mother's children; Because zeal for Your house has eaten me up, And the reproaches of those who reproach You have fallen on me.

John 7:3–5: "His brothers therefore said to Him, 'Depart from here and go into Judea, that Your disciples also may see the works that You are doing. For no one does anything in secret while he him- self seeks to be known openly. If You do these things, show Yourself to the world.' For even His brothers did not believe in Him.

Psalm 69:9: "Because zeal for Your house has eaten me up, And the reproaches of those who reproach You have fallen on me."

John 2:17: "Then His disciples remembered that it was written, 'Zeal for Your house has eaten Me up.'"

Psalm 69:20–22: "Reproach has broken my heart and I am full of heaviness; I looked for someone to take pity, but there was none; And for comforters, but I found none. They also gave me gall for my food and for my thirst they gave me vinegar to drink. Let their table become a snare before them, And their well-being a trap."

Matthew 27:34: "They gave Him sour wine mingled with gall to drink. But when He had tasted it, He would not drink."

Psalm 72:10–11: "The kings of Tarshish and of the isles Will bring presents; The kings of Sheba and Seba Will offer gifts. Yes, all kings shall fall down before Him; All nations shall serve Him."

Matthew 2:9-11 When they heard the king, they departed; and behold, the star which they had seen in the East went before them, till it came and stood over where the young Child was. When they saw the star, they rejoiced with exceedingly great joy. And when they had come into the house, they saw the young Child with Mary, His mother, and fell down and worshiped Him. And when they had opened their treasures, they presented gifts to Him: gold, frankincense, and myrrh."

Psalm 72:12–14: "For He will deliver the needy when he cries, the poor also, and him who has no helper. He will spare the poor and needy and will save the souls of the needy. He will redeem their life from oppression and violence; And precious shall be their blood in His sight."

Luke 7:22: "Jesus answered and said to them, 'Go and tell John the things you have seen and heard that the blind see, the lame walk, the lepers are cleansed, the deaf hear, the dead are raised, the poor have the gospel preached to them.'"

Psalm 78:2: "I will open my mouth in a parable; I will utter dark sayings of old."

Matt 13:10- 15 And the disciples came and said to Him, "Why do You speak to them in parables?" 11 He answered and said to them, "Because it has been given to you to know the mysteries of the kingdom of heaven, but to them it has not been given.12 For whoever has, to him more will be given, and he will have abundance; but whoever does not have, even what he has will be taken away from him.13 Therefore I speak to them in parables, because seeing they do not see, and hearing they do not hear, nor do they understand.14 And in them the prophecy of Isaiah is fulfilled, which says: 'Hearing you will hear and shall not understand, And seeing you will see and not perceive; 15 For the hearts of this people have grown dull. Their ears are hard of hearing, and their eyes they have closed, lest they should see with their eyes and hear with their ears,

Lest they should understand with their hearts and turn, **So that I should heal them.**'

Psalm 109:4: "In return for my love they are my accusers, But I give myself to prayer."

Matthew 5:44: "But I say to you, love your enemies, bless those who curse you, do good to those who hate you, and pray for those who spitefully use you and persecute you."

Luke 23:34: "Then Jesus said, 'Father, forgive them, for they do not know what they do.'"

Psalm 110:4: "The Lord has sworn and will not relent, 'You are a priest forever According to the order of Melchizedek.'"

Hebrews 5:1–6: "For every high priest taken from among men is appointed for men in things pertaining to God, that he may offer both gifts and sacrifices for sins. He can have compassion on those who are ignorant and going astray, since he himself is also subject to weakness. Because of this he is required as for the people, so also for himself, to offer sacrifices for sins. And no man takes this honor to himself, but he who is called by God, just as Aaron was. A Priest Forever So also Christ did not glorify Himself to become High Priest, but it was He who said to Him: 'You are My Son, Today I have begotten You.' As He also says in another place: 'You are a priest forever According to the order of Melchizedek.'"

Hebrews 6:20: "Where the forerunner has entered for us, even Jesus, having become High Priest forever according to the order of Melchizedek."

Hebrews 7:15–17: "And it is yet far more evident if, in the like- ness of Melchizedek, there arises another priest who has come, not accord- ing to the law of a fleshly commandment, but according to the power of an endless life. For He testifies: '"You are a priest forever According to the order of Melchizedek.'"

Psalm 118:22–23: "The stone which the builders rejected Has be- come the chief cornerstone. This was the Lord's doing; It is marvelous in our eyes."

Matt 21:42 Jesus said to them, "Have you never read in the Scriptures: 'The stone which the builders rejected Has become the chief cornerstone. This was the Lord's doing, And it is marvelous in our eyes'?

Isa 6:9-10 And He said, "Go, and tell this people: 'Keep on hearing, but do not understand.

Keep on seeing, but do not perceive.' 10 "Make the heart of this people dull, and their ears heavy, and shut their eyes; Lest they see with their eyes, and hear with their ears, And understand with their heart, And **return and be healed.**"

Matthew 13:13–15: "Therefore I speak to them in parables, because seeing they do not see, and hearing they do not hear, nor do they understand. And in them the prophecy of Isaiah is fulfilled, which says: 'Hearing you will hear and shall not understand and seeing you will see and not perceive; For the hearts of this people have grown dull. Their ears are hard of hearing, and their eyes they have closed, lest they should see with their eyes and hear with their ears, lest they should understand with their hearts and turn, **so that I should heal them.**'"

John 12:37–40: "But although He had done so many signs before them, they did not believe in Him, that the word of Isaiah the prophet might be fulfilled, which he spoke: 'Lord, who has believed our report? And to whom has the arm of the Lord been revealed?' Therefore, they could not believe, because Isaiah said again: 'He has blinded their eyes and hardened their hearts, lest they should see with their eyes, lest they should understand with their hearts and turn, **So that I should heal them.**'"

Acts 28:24–27: "And some were persuaded by the things which were spoken, and some disbelieved. So, when they did not agree among themselves, they departed after Paul had said one word: 'The Holy Spirit spoke rightly through Isaiah the prophet to our fathers, saying, "Go to this people and say: 'Hearing you will hear, and shall not understand; And seeing you will see, and not perceive; For the hearts of this people have grown dull. Their ears are hard of hearing and their eyes they have closed, lest they should see with their eyes and hear with their ears, lest they should understand with their hearts and turn, **So that I should heal them.**'"

Isaiah 7:13–14: "Then he said, 'Hear now, O house of David! Is it a small thing for you to weary men, but will you weary my God also? Therefore, the Lord Himself will give you a sign: Behold, the virgin shall conceive and bear a Son, and shall call His name Immanuel.'"

Matthew 1:18–23: "Now the birth of Jesus Christ was as follows: After His mother Mary was betrothed to Joseph, before they came together, she was found with child of the Holy Spirit. Then Joseph her husband, being a just man, and not wanting to make her a public example, was minded to put her away secretly. But while he thought about these things, behold, an angel of the Lord appeared to him in a dream, saying, 'Joseph, son of David, do not be afraid to take to you Mary your wife, for that which is conceived in her is of the Holy Spirit. And she will bring forth a Son, and you shall call His name Jesus, for He will save His people from their sins.' So, all this was done that it might be fulfilled which was spoken by the Lord through the prophet, saying: 'Behold, the virgin shall be with child, and bear a Son, and they shall call His name Immanuel,' which is translated, 'God with us.'"

Luke 1:26–35: "Now in the sixth month the angel Gabriel was sent by God to a city of Galilee named Nazareth, to a virgin betrothed to a man whose name was Joseph, of the house of David. The virgin's name was Mary. And having come in, the angel said to her, 'Rejoice, highly favored one, the Lord is with you; blessed are you among women!' But when she saw him, she was troubled at his saying, and considered what manner of greeting this was. Then the angel said to her, 'Do not be afraid, Mary, for you have found favor with God. And behold, you will conceive in your womb and bring forth a Son and shall call His name Jesus. He will be great and will be called the Son of the Highest; and the Lord God will give Him the throne of His father David. And He will reign over the house of Jacob forever, and of His kingdom there will be no end.' Then Mary said to the angel, 'How can this be, since I do not know a man?' And the angel answered and said to her, "The Holy Spirit will come upon you, and the power of the Highest will overshadow you; therefore, also, that Holy One who is to be born will be called the Son of God.

Isaiah 8:14: "He will be as a sanctuary, But a stone of stumbling and a rock of offense to both the houses of Israel, As a trap and a snare to the inhabitants of Jerusalem."

Romans 9:31–33: "But Israel, pursuing the law of righteous- ness, has not attained to the law of righteousness. Why? Because they did not seek it by faith, but as it were, by the works of the law. For they stumbled at that stumbling stone. As it is written: 'Behold, I lay in Zion a stumbling stone and rock of offense, and whoever believes on Him will not be put to shame.'"

First Peter 2:7–8: "Therefore, to you who believe, He is precious; but to those who are disobedient, 'The stone which the builders re- jected Has become the chief cornerstone,' and 'A stone of stum- bling and a rock of offense.' They stumble, being disobedient to the word, to which they also were appointed."

Isaiah 9:1–2: "Nevertheless the gloom will not be upon her who is distressed, as when at first, He lightly esteemed the land of Zebulun and the land of Naphtali, and afterward more heavily oppressed her, By the way of the sea, beyond the Jordan, In Galilee of the Gentiles. The people who walked in darkness Have seen a great light; Those who dwelt in the land of the shadow of death, upon them a light has shined."

Matthew 4:12–16: "Now when Jesus heard that John had been put in prison, He departed to Galilee. And leaving Nazareth, He came and dwelt in Capernaum, which is by the sea, in the regions of Zebulun and Naphtali, that it might be fulfilled which was spoken by Isaiah the prophet, saying: 'The land of Zebulun and the land of Naphtali, By the way of the sea, beyond the Jordan, Galilee of the Gentiles: The people who sat in darkness have seen a great light, And upon those who sat in the region and shadow of death Light has dawned.

Isaiah 9:6: "For unto us a Child is born, unto us a Son is given; And the government will be upon His shoulder. And His name will be called Wonderful, Counselor, Mighty God, Everlasting Father, Prince of Peace."

Isaiah 9:7: "Of the increase of His government and peace There will be no end, Upon the throne of David and over His kingdom, To order it and establish it with judgment and justice from that time forward, even forever. The zeal of the Lord of hosts will perform this."

Luke 2:11: "For there is born to you this day in the city of David a Savior, who is Christ the Lord."

Matthew 1:1: "The book of the genealogy of Jesus Christ, the Son of David, the Son of Abraham."

Luke 1:32: "He will be great and will be called the Son of the Highest; and the Lord God will give Him the throne of His father David."

Luke 2:11: "For there is born to you this day in the city of David a Savior, who is Christ the Lord."

Acts 13:22–23: "And when He had removed him, He raised up for them David as king, to whom also He gave testimony and said, 'I have found David the son of Jesse, a man after My own heart, who will do all My will.' From this man's seed, according to the promise, God raised up for Israel a Savior—Jesus."

Isaiah 11:1–2: "There shall come forth a Rod from the stem of Jesse and a Branch shall grow out of his roots. The Spirit of the Lord shall rest upon Him, The Spirit of wisdom and understanding, The Spirit of counsel and might, The Spirit of knowledge and of the fear of the Lord."

Matthew 1:6: "And Jesse begot David the king."

Acts 13:22–23: "And when He had removed him, He raised up for them David as king, to whom also He gave testimony and said, 'I have found David the son of Jesse, a man after My own heart, who will do all My will.' From this man's seed, according to the promise, God raised up for Israel a Savior—Jesus.

Isaiah 11:2: "The Spirit of the Lord shall rest upon Him, The Spirit of wisdom and understanding, The Spirit of counsel and might,

The Spirit of knowledge and of the fear of the Lord."

Matthew 3:16: "When He had been baptized, Jesus came up immediately from the water; and behold, the heavens were opened to Him, and He saw the Spirit of God descending like a dove and alighting upon Him."

Mark 1:10: "And immediately, coming up from the water, He saw the heavens parting and the Spirit descending upon Him like a dove.

Luke 3:22: "And the Holy Spirit descended in bodily form like a dove upon Him, and a voice came from heaven which said, 'You are My beloved Son; in You I am well pleased.'"

Luke 4:18: "'The Spirit of the Lord is upon Me, Because He has anointed Me To preach the gospel to the poor; He has sent Me to heal the brokenhearted, to proclaim liberty to the captives and recovery of sight to the blind to set at liberty those who are oppressed.'"

John 1:32: "And John bore witness, saying, 'I saw the Spirit descending from heaven like a dove, and He remained upon Him.'"

John 3:34: "For He whom God has sent speaks the words of God, for God does not give the Spirit by measure."

Acts 10:38: "How God anointed Jesus of Nazareth with the Holy Spirit and with power, who went about doing good and healing all who were oppressed by the devil, for God was with Him."

Isaiah 29:18: "In that day the deaf shall hear the words of the book, And the eyes of the blind shall see out of obscurity and out of darkness."

Matthew 11:5: "The blind see and the lame walk; the lepers are cleansed and the deaf hear; the dead are raised up and the poor have the gospel preached to them."

John 9:39: "And Jesus said, 'For judgment I have come into this world, that those who do not see may see, and that those who see may be made blind.'"

Luke 7:19-23 And John, calling two of his disciples to him, sent them to Jesus, saying, "Are You the Coming One, or do we look for another?" 20 When the men had come to Him, they said, "John the Baptist has sent us to You, saying, 'Are You the Coming One, or do we look for another?'" 21 And that very hour He cured many of infirmities, afflictions, and evil spirits; and to many blind He gave sight. 22 Jesus answered and said to them, "Go and tell John the things you have seen and heard: that the blind see, the lame walk, the lepers are cleansed, the deaf hear, the dead are raised, the poor have the gospel preached to them.23 And blessed is he who is not offended because of Me."

Mark 7:37: "And they were astonished beyond measure, saying, 'He has done all things well. He makes both the deaf to hear and the mute to speak.'"

Isaiah 35:4–6: "Say to those who are fearful-hearted, 'Be strong, do not fear! Behold, your God will come with vengeance, With the recompense of God; He will come and save you.' Then the eyes of the blind shall be opened, And the ears of the deaf shall be unstopped. Then the lame shall leap like a deer and the tongue of the dumb sing. For waters shall burst forth in the wilderness, And streams in the desert."

Matthew 9:30: "And their eyes were opened. And Jesus sternly warned them, saying, 'See that no one knows it.'"

Matthew 11:4–6: "Jesus answered and said to them, 'Go and tell John the things which you hear and see: The blind see and the lame walk; the lepers are cleansed and the deaf hear; the dead are raised up and the poor have the gospel preached to them. And blessed is he who is not offended because of Me.'"

Matthew 12:22: "Then one was brought to Him who was demon-possessed, blind and mute; and He healed him, so that the blind and mute man both spoke and saw."

Matthew 20:34: "So Jesus had compassion and touched their eyes. And immediately their eyes received sight, and they followed Him."

Matthew 21:14: "Then the blind and the lame came to Him in the temple, and He healed them."

Mark 7:32-35 Then they brought to Him one who was deaf and had an impediment in his speech, and they begged Him to put His hand on him. 33 And He took him aside from the multitude, and put His fingers in his ears, and He spat and touched his tongue. 34 Then, looking up to heaven, He sighed, and said to him, "Ephphatha," that is, "Be opened. "Immediately his ears were opened, and the impediment of his tongue was loosed, and he spoke plainly.

John 9:1–7: "Now as Jesus passed by, He saw a man who was blind from birth. And His disciples asked Him, saying, 'Rabbi, who sinned, this man or his parents, that he was born blind?' Jesus answered, 'Neither this man nor his parents sinned, but that the works of God should be revealed in him. I must work the works of Him who sent Me while it is day; the night is coming when no one can work. As long as I am in the world, I am the light of the world.' When He had said these things, He spat on the ground and made clay with the saliva; and He anointed the eyes of the blind man with the clay. And He said to him, 'Go, wash in the pool of Siloam (which is translated, Sent).' So, he went and washed, and came back seeing."

John 11:47: "Then the chief priests and the Pharisees gathered a council and said, 'What shall we do? For this Man works many signs.'"

Isaiah 40:3–4: "The voice of one crying in the wilderness: 'Prepare the way of the Lord; Make straight in the desert A highway for our God. Every valley shall be exalted, and every mountain and hill brought low; The crooked places shall be made straight and the rough places smooth."

Matthew 3:3: "For this is he who was spoken of by the prophet Isaiah, saying: 'The voice of one crying in the wilderness: "Prepare the way of the Lord; Make His paths straight."'"

Mark 1:3: "'The voice of one crying in the wilderness: "Prepare the way of the Lord; Make His paths straight."'"

Luke 3:3-4 And he went into all the region around the Jordan, preaching a baptism of repentance for the remission of sins, 4 as it is written in the book of the words of Isaiah the prophet, saying: "The voice of one crying in the wilderness: 'Prepare the way of the Lord; Make His paths straight. 5 Every valley shall be filled, and every mountain and hill brought low; The crooked places shall be made straight And the rough ways smooth; 6 And all flesh shall see the salvation of God.'"

John 1:23: "He said: 'I am "The voice of one crying in the wilderness: 'Make straight the way of the Lord,'" as the prophet Isaiah said.'"

Isaiah 40:10–11: "Behold, the Lord God shall come with a strong hand, And His arm shall rule for Him; Behold, His reward is with Him, And His work before Him. He will feed His flock like a shepherd; He will gather the lambs with His arm, and carry them in His bosom, and gently lead those who are with young."

John 10:11: "'I am the good shepherd. The good shepherd gives His life for the sheep.'"

Hebrews 13:20: "Now may the God of peace who brought up our Lord Jesus from the dead, that great Shepherd of the sheep, through the blood of the everlasting covenant."

First Peter 2:25: "For you were like sheep going astray but have now returned to the Shepherd and Overseer of your souls."

Isaiah 42:1–4: "'Behold! My Servant whom I uphold, My Elect One in whom My soul delights! I have put My Spirit upon Him; He will bring forth justice to the Gentiles. He will not cry out, nor raise His voice, nor cause His voice to be heard in the street. A bruised reed He will not break and smoking flax He will not quench; He will bring forth justice for truth. He will not fail nor be discouraged, Till He has established justice in the earth; And the coastlands shall wait for His law.'"

Matt 12:16-17 Yet He warned them not to make Him known, 17 that it might be fulfilled which was spoken by Isaiah the prophet, saying: 18 "Behold! My Servant whom I have chosen, My Beloved in whom My soul is well pleased! I will put My Spirit upon Him, And He will declare justice to the Gentiles. 19 He will not quarrel nor cry out, nor will anyone hear His voice in the streets. 20 A bruised reed He will not break, and smoking flax He will not quench, Till He sends forth justice to victory; 21 And in His name Gentiles will trust."

Isaiah 42:6: "'I, the Lord, have called You in righteousness and will hold Your hand; I will keep You and give You as a covenant to the people, As a light to the Gentiles.'"

Luke 2:25–32: "And behold, there was a man in Jerusalem whose name was Simeon, and this man was just and devout, waiting for the Consolation of Israel, and the Holy Spirit was upon him. And it had been revealed to him by the Holy Spirit that he would not see death before he had seen the Lord's Christ. So he came by the Spirit into the temple. And when the parents brought in the Child Jesus, to do for Him according to the custom of the law, he took Him up in his arms and blessed God and said: 'Lord, now You are letting Your servant depart in peace, According to Your word; For my eyes have seen Your salvation Which You have prepared before the face of all peoples, A light to bring revelation to the Gentiles, And the glory of Your people Israel.'"

Acts 26:23: "'That the Christ would suffer, that He would be the first to rise from the dead and would proclaim light to the Jewish people and to the Gentiles.'"

Isaiah 50:6: "I gave My back to those who struck Me, And My cheeks to those who plucked out the beard; I did not hide My face from shame and spitting."

Matthew 26:67–68: "Then they spat in His face and beat Him; and others struck Him with the palms of their hands, saying, 'Prophesy to us, Christ! Who is the one who struck You?'"

Matt 27:26 Then he released Barabbas to them; and when he had scourged Jesus, he delivered Him to be crucified. 27 Then the soldiers of the governor took Jesus into the Praetorium and gathered the whole garrison around Him. 28 And they stripped Him and put a scarlet robe on Him. 29 When they had twisted a crown of thorns, they put it on His head, and a reed in His right hand. And they bowed the knee before Him and mocked Him, saying, "Hail, King of the Jews!"

Mark 14:65: "Then some began to spit on Him, and to blind- fold Him, and to beat Him, and to say to Him, 'Prophesy!' And the officers struck Him with the palms of their hands."

Mark 15:15–19: "So Pilate, wanting to gratify the crowd, released Barabbas to them; and he delivered Jesus, after he had scourged Him, to be crucified. The Soldiers Mock Jesus Then the soldiers led Him away into the hall called Praetorium, and they called together the whole garrison. And they clothed Him with purple; and they twisted a crown of thorns, put it on His head, and began to salute Him, 'Hail, King of the Jews!' Then they struck Him on the head with a reed and spat on Him; and bowing the knee, they worshiped Him."

Luke 22:63–65: "Now the men who held Jesus mocked Him and beat Him. And having blindfolded Him, they struck Him on the face and asked Him, saying, 'Prophesy! Who is the one who struck You?' And many other things they blasphemously spoke against Him."

John 19:1: "So then Pilate took Jesus and scourged Him."

Isaiah 55:4–5: "Indeed I have given him as a witness to the people, A leader and commander for the people. Surely you shall call a nation you do not know and nations who do not know you shall run to you, Because of the Lord your God, And the Holy One of Israel; For He has glorified you.'"

Romans 9:23–26: "And that He might make known the riches of His glory on the vessels of mercy, which He had prepared before- hand for glory, even us whom He called, not of the Jews only, but also of the Gentiles? As He says also in Hosea: 'I will call them My people, who were not My people, and her beloved, who was not beloved.' 'And it shall come to pass in the place where it was said to them, "You are not My people," There they shall be called sons of the living God.'"

Isaiah 59:20: "The Redeemer will come to Zion and to those who turn from transgression in Jacob,' Says the Lord.

Romans 11:26–27: "And so all Israel will be saved, as it is writ- ten: 'The Deliverer will come out of Zion, And He will turn away ungodli- ness from Jacob; For this is My covenant with them, When I take away their sins.

Isaiah 61:1–2: "'The Spirit of the Lord God is upon Me, Because the Lord has anointed Me To preach good tidings to the poor; He has sent Me to heal the brokenhearted to proclaim liberty to the captives, and the opening of the prison to those who are bound; To proclaim the acceptable year of the Lord, And the day of vengeance of our God; To comfort all who mourn.'"

Luke 4:16–21: "So He came to Nazareth, where He had been brought up. And as His custom was, He went into the synagogue on the Sabbath day, and stood up to read. And He was handed the book of the prophet Isaiah. And when He had opened the book, He found the place where it was written: 'The Spirit of the Lord is upon Me, Because He has anointed Me To preach the gospel to the poor; He has sent Me to heal the brokenhearted, To proclaim, liberty to the captives And recovery of sight to the blind, To set at liberty those who are oppressed; To proclaim the acceptable year of the Lord.' Then He closed the book and gave it back to the attendant and sat down. And the eyes of all who were in the synagogue were fixed on Him. And He began to say to them, 'Today this Scripture is fulfilled in your hearing.'"

Acts 10:38: "How God anointed Jesus of Nazareth with the Holy Spirit and with power, who went about doing good and healing all who were oppressed by the devil, for God was with Him."

Jer 31:15 Thus says the Lord: "A voice was heard in Ramah, Lamentation and bitter weeping, Rachel weeping for her children, refusing to be comforted for her children, Because they are no more.

Matthew 2:16: "Then Herod, when he saw that he was deceived by the wise men, was exceedingly angry; and he sent forth and put to death all the male children who were in Bethlehem and in all its districts, from two years old and under, according to the time which he had determined from the wise men."

Jeremiah 31:31–34: "'Behold, the days are coming,' says the Lord, 'when I will make a new covenant with the house of Israel and with the house of Judah—not according to the covenant that I made with their fathers in the day that I took them by the hand to lead them out of the land of Egypt, My covenant which they broke, though I was a husband to them,' says the Lord. 'But this is the covenant that I will make with the house of Israel after those days,' says the Lord: 'I will put My law in their minds and write it on their hearts; and I will be their God, and they shall be My people. No more shall every man teach his neighbor, and every man his brother, saying, "Know the Lord," for they all shall know Me, from the least of them to the greatest of them,' says the Lord. 'For I will forgive their iniquity, and their sin I will remember no more.'"

Jeremiah 32:37–40: "Behold, I will gather them out of all countries where I have driven them in My anger, in My fury, and in great wrath; I will bring them back to this place, and I will cause them to dwell safely. They shall be My people, and I will be their God; then I will give them one heart and one way, that they may fear Me forever, for the good of them and their children after them. And I will make an everlasting covenant with them, that I will not turn away from doing them good; but I will put My fear in their hearts so that they will not depart from Me."

Luke 22:15-20Then He said to them, "With fervent desire I have desired to eat this Passover with you before I suffer;16 for I say to you, I will no longer eat of it until it is fulfilled in the kingdom of God." 17 Then He took the cup, and gave thanks, and said, "Take this and divide it among yourselves;18 for I say to you, I will not drink of the fruit of the vine until the kingdom of God comes." 19 And He took bread, gave thanks and broke it, and gave it to them, saying, "This is My body which is given for you; do this in remembrance of Me." 20 Likewise He also took the cup after supper, saying, "This cup is the new covenant in My blood, which is shed for you.

Hebrews 10:15–20: "But the Holy Spirit also witnesses to us; for after He had said before, 'This is the covenant that I will make with them after those days, says the Lord: I will put My laws into their hearts, and in their minds, I will write them,' then He adds, 'Their sins and their lawless deeds I will remember no more.' Now where there is remission of these, there is no longer an offering for sin. Therefore, brethren, having boldness to enter the Holiest by the blood of Jesus, by a new and living way which He consecrated for us, through the veil, that is, His flesh."

Hosea 2:23: "Then I will sow her for Myself in the earth, and I will have mercy on her who had not obtained mercy; Then I will say to those who were not My people, 'You are My people!' And they shall say, 'You are my God!'"

Romans 9:23–26: "And that He might make known the riches of His glory on the vessels of mercy, which He had prepared before- hand for glory, even us whom He called, not of the Jews only, but also of the Gentiles? As He says also in Hosea: 'I will call them My people, who were not My people, and her beloved, who was not beloved.' 'And it shall come to pass in the place where it was said to them, "You are not My people," There they shall be called sons of the living God.'"

Hosea 11:1: "'When Israel was a child, I loved him and out of Egypt I called My son.'"

Matthew 2:13–15: "Now when they had departed, behold, an angel of the Lord appeared to Joseph in a dream, saying, 'Arise, take the young Child and His mother, flee to Egypt, and stay there until I bring you word; for Herod will seek the young Child to destroy Him.' When he arose, he took the young Child and His mother by night and departed for Egypt, and was there until the death of Herod, that it might be fulfilled which was spoken by the Lord through the prophet, saying, 'Out of Egypt I called My Son.

Joel 2:28–32: "'And it shall come to pass afterward That I will pour out My Spirit on all flesh; Your sons and your daughters shall prophesy, your old men shall dream dreams, your young men shall see visions. And also, on My menservants and on My maid servants I will pour out My Spirit in those days. "And I will show wonders in the heavens and in the earth: Blood and fire and pillars of smoke. The sun shall be turned into darkness, And the moon into blood, Before the coming of the great and awesome day of the Lord. And it shall come to pass That whoever calls on the name of the Lord Shall be saved. For in Mount Zion and in Jerusalem there shall be deliverance, As the Lord has said, Among the remnant whom the Lord calls.'"

Acts 2:16–23: "But this is what was spoken by the prophet Joel: 'And it shall come to pass in the last days, says God, That I will pour out of My Spirit on all flesh; your sons and your daughters shall prophesy, your young men shall see visions, your old men shall dream dreams. And on My menservants and on My maid servants I will pour out My Spirit in those days; And they shall prophesy. I will show wonders in heaven above and signs in the earth beneath: Blood and fire and vapor of smoke. The sun shall be turned into darkness, And the moon into blood before the coming of the great and awe- some day of the Lord. And it shall come to pass That whoever calls on the name of the Lord Shall be saved.' 'Men of Israel, hear these words: Jesus of Nazareth, a Man attested by God to you by miracles, wonders, and signs which God did through Him in your midst, as you yourselves also know—Him, being delivered by the determined purpose and foreknowledge of God, you have taken by lawless hands, have crucified, and put to death.'"

Amos 9:11–12: "On that day I will raise up the tabernacle of David, which has fallen down and repair its damages. I will raise up its ruins and rebuild it as in the days of old; That they may possess the remnant of Edom and all the Gentiles who are called by My name,' says the Lord who does this thing.

Acts 15:16–18: "After! this I will return and will rebuild the tabernacle of David, which has fallen down; I will rebuild its ruins, And I will set it up; So that the rest of mankind may seek the Lord, even all the Gentiles who are called by My name,' Says the Lord who does all these things. 'Known to God from eternity are all His works.'

Micah 5:1: "Now gather yourself in troops, O daughter of troops; He has laid siege against us; They will strike the judge of Israel with a rod on the cheek."

Matthew 27:30: "Then they spat on Him and took the reed and struck Him on the head."

Micah 5:2–5: "'But you, Bethlehem Ephrathah, though you are little among the thousands of Judah yet out of you shall come forth to Me the One to be Ruler in Israel, whose goings forth are from of old, from everlasting.' Therefore He shall give them up, Until the time that she who is in labor has given birth; Then the remnant of His brethren Shall return to the children of Israel. And He shall stand and feed His flock in the strength of the Lord, In the majesty of the name of the Lord His God and they shall abide, for now He shall be great to the ends of the earth; And this One shall be peace. Judgment on Israel's Enemies When the Assyrian comes into our land and when he treads in our palaces, then we will raise against him Seven shepherds and eight princely men."

Matthew 2:1–6: "Now after Jesus was born in Bethlehem of Judea in the days of Herod the king, behold, wise men from the East came to Jerusalem, saying, 'Where is He who has been born King of the Jews? For we have seen His star in the East and have come to worship Him.' When Herod the king heard this, he was troubled, and all Jerusalem with him. And when he had gathered all the chief priests and scribes of the people together, he inquired of them where the Christ was to be born. So, they said to him, 'In Bethlehem of Judea, for thus it is written by the prophet: "But you, Bethlehem, in the land of Judah are not the least among the rulers of Judah for out of you shall come a Ruler Who will shepherd My people, Israel."

Zechariah 2:10–13: "'Sing and rejoice, O daughter of Zion! For behold, I am coming, and I will dwell in your midst,' says the Lord. 'Many nations shall be joined to the Lord in that day, and they shall become My people. And I will dwell in your midst. Then you will know that the Lord of hosts has sent Me to you. And the Lord will take possession of Judah as His inheritance in the Holy Land and will again choose Jerusalem. Be silent, all flesh, before the Lord, for He is aroused from His holy habitation!'"

John 1:14: "And the Word became flesh and dwelt among us, and we beheld His glory, the glory as of the only begotten of the Father, full of grace and truth."

Revelation 21:3: "And I heard a loud voice from heaven saying, 'Behold, the tabernacle of God is with men, and He will dwell with them, and they shall be His people. God Himself will be with them and be their God.'"

Zechariah 9:9: "'Rejoice greatly, O daughter of Zion! Shout, O daughter of Jerusalem! Behold, your King is coming to you; He is just and having salvation, Lowly and riding on a donkey, A colt, the foal of a donkey.'"

Mark 11:1–10: "Now when they drew near Jerusalem, to Bethphage and Bethany, at the Mount of Olives, He sent two of His disciples; and He said to them, 'Go into the village opposite you; and as soon as you have entered it you will find a colt tied, on which no one has sat. Loose it and bring it. And if anyone says to you, "Why are you doing this?" say, "The Lord has need of it," and immediately he will send it here.' So, they went their way, and found the colt tied by the door outside on the street, and they loosed it. But some of those who stood there said to them, 'What are you doing loosing the colt?' And they spoke to them just as Jesus had commanded. So, they let them go. Then they brought the colt to Jesus and threw their clothes on it, and He sat on it. And many spread their clothes on the road, and others cut down leafy branches from the trees and spread them on the road. Then those who went before and those who followed cried out, saying: 'Hosanna! "Blessed is He who comes in the name of the Lord!" Blessed is the kingdom of our father David That comes in the name of the Lord! Hosanna in the highest.

Matthew 21:1–5: "Now when they drew near Jerusalem, and came to Bethphage, at the Mount of Olives, then Jesus sent two disciples, saying to them, 'Go into the village opposite you, and immediately you will find a donkey tied, and a colt with her. Loose them and bring them to Me. And if anyone says anything to you, you shall say, "The Lord has need of them," and immediately he will send them.' All this was done that it might be fulfilled which was spoken by the prophet, saying: 'Tell the daughter of Zion, "Behold, your King is coming to you, Lowly, and sitting on a donkey, A colt, the foal of a donkey."'"

John 12:14–15: "Then Jesus, when He had found a young donkey, sat on it; as it is written: 'Fear not, daughter of Zion; Behold, your King is coming, Sitting on a donkey's colt.'"

Malachi 4:5–6: "'Behold, I will send you Elijah the prophet Before the coming of the great and dreadful day of the Lord. And he will turn the hearts of the fathers to the children, And the hearts of the children to their fathers, Lest I come and strike the earth with a curse.

Matthew 11:13–14: "For all the prophets and the law prophesied until John. And if you are willing to receive it, he is Elijah who is to come."

Mark 9:11–13: "And they asked Him, saying, 'Why do the scribes say that Elijah must come first?' Then He answered and told them, 'Indeed, Elijah is coming first and restores all things. And how is it writ- ten concerning the Son of Man, that He must suffer many things and be treated with contempt? But I say to you that Elijah has also come, and they did to him whatever they wished, as it is written of him.'"

Luke 1:17: "'He will also go before Him in the spirit and power of Elijah, "to turn the hearts of the fathers to the children," and the disobedient to the wisdom of the just, to make ready a people pre- pared for the Lord.'"

Luke 7:27–28: "'This is he of whom it is written: "Behold, I send My messenger before Your face, Who will prepare Your way before You." For I say to you, among those born of women there is not a greater prophet than John the Baptist; but he who is least in the kingdom of God is greater than he.'"

<u>Please send your review to the company you bought this from</u> **to help us come together**. <u>This wolf hunter for Jesus will close with "I love you" and look forward to spending eternity with you, and the Messiah, Yeshua, Jesus and our Father the living God.</u>

Receive Jesus now or again to confirm you have!

Pray with your voice so you hear yourself. If no voice, God always hears your heart!

Dear God,

I know that I am a sinner. I want to turn away from my sins and ask for your forgiveness. I believe that Jesus Christ is your son. I believe he died for my sins and that you raised him to life. I want him to come into my heart. I want to trust Jesus as my Savior and follow him as my Lord from this day forward. I ask in Your Son Jesus's name.

Amen, which means, so be it!

Date _____ Signature _____

www.ingramcontent.com/pod-product-compliance
Lightning Source LLC
Chambersburg PA
CBHW060537130626
46553CB00002B/796